THE THRONE IS NO GAME

HIS OR YOUR KINGDOM COME?

DR. RON MORRISON

urbanpress

The Throne is No Game
by Dr. Ron Morrison
Copyright © 2019 Dr. Ron Morrison

ISBN # 978-1-63360-113-0

All rights reserved under International Copyright Law. Written permission must be secured from the publisher/author to reproduce, copy, or transmit any part of this book.

Unless otherwise noted, all scripture quotations taken from the Holy Bible from the NEW KING JAMES VERSION (NKJV): Scripture taken from the NEW KING JAMES VERSION®. Copyright© 1982 by Thomas Nelson, Inc. Used by permission. All rights reserved.

For Worldwide Distribution Printed in the U.S.A.

Urban Press
P.O. Box 8881
Pittsburgh, PA 15221-0881 USA
412.646.2780
www.urbanpress.us

DEDICATION

My bride Anita. Thank you for helping me grow in Christ these past 40 years. It has been a blessing to share life together with you, and grateful that it will last throughout eternity because of our Lord Jesus Christ.

My family at Hope Alliance Bible Church. It has been a joy to serve as your pastor, as together we have been developing disciples who live and love like Jesus.

My Moody Bible Institute students and radio family of WCRF in Cleveland. You have made me a better teacher and student of the Scriptures.

My teammates in the Christian and Missionary Alliance. Let's keep working together until every people group is reached with the gospel.

TABLE OF CONTENTS

PROLOGUE

When Mary sang her song of praise as she learned of her miraculous pregnancy, she said,

> "He has shown strength with His arm, He has scattered the proud in the imagination of their hearts. He has put down the mighty from their thrones, and exalted the lowly" (Luke 1:51-52).

There has always been a certain fascination with thrones. Most people seem to want one or live as though they are somehow reigning and ruling from one. *Game of Thrones* is a wildly popular show in our day. On it, families fight for honor and the right to sit on the Iron Throne, deploying witches and dragons and utilizing betrayal and conspiracies, shifting alliances and breaking promises, all with the goal of gaining more power. In real life, wars are fought and lives are lost as men and women fight for access to power, often represented best by a throne with a title.

Mary's inspired words remind us that our Lord has a way of taking down those persons who seek to exalt themselves on the thrones of this worldly system. When all is said and done, the Lord alone will manifest His rule from His throne (see Revelation 3:21) and be surrounded by worshipers (see Revelation 4:4). Even now we can boldly and confidently come to His throne of grace to find help in our time of need (see Hebrews 4:16).

It is not only nations and families that seek the throne, however. We all sit on the throne of our own lives, running things as we see fit, until we come face to face with our inability to do so in a way that produces peace and happiness. Some people never abdicate the throne of their own lives, but others do and allow One to sit there who is omnipotent and omniscient—the Lord Jesus Christ. Even after they make that decision to surrender their throne, it requires a lifetime of decisions to stay off the throne and allow God to rule and reign in every area of their lives.

In this book, we are going to learn "throne lessons" from the lives of two kings of Israel and Judah—Saul and David. We will see examples of all that can go wrong when men do not re-alize who is really the One who has a right to be on the throne. Israel wanted a visible king to lead them into battle, just like the other nations had (see 1 Samuel 8:4-5). That desire was a tragic rejection of the invisible King who was ruling over them, and they suffered the consequences of that short-sighted request. As you read the following pages, my prayer is that you will choose to turn over the throne of your life to the One who is best suited to reign and rule, the Lord Jesus Christ. That throne is not a game but a serious matter, for you like every other person in the world must answer the question where the throne is concerned: *His or your Kingdom?*

Dr. Ron Morrison

INTRODUCTION

The lives of King Saul and King David have been the subject of countless Bible studies, books, and sermons over the years. What else can possibly be said about them? Why would someone choose such familiar ground for yet another book?

My preparation for ministry began in the early 1980s. I was working swing shifts at a factory, well-paid, married, and in my thirties. Going away to school was not an option. I enrolled in distance learning classes from Moody Bible Institute and this was back in the days when lessons and exams were snail mailed. We eagerly awaited the return mail to see if we had learned our lessons well. Handwriting and typing were the two options, and white-out was close at hand to fix typing errors.

The first class I took was on First Samuel and the life of King David. It was fascinating to learn life lessons from stories other than David and Goliath. The call of God often leads to a journey of preparation for leadership and character development, accompanied by painful encounters that may not make sense until the leader is finally positioned to lead. The lessons should never stop, but hopefully a wiser perspective has been obtained that helps make each bump in the road educational rather than harmful.

As you read the pages that follow, I trust you come with the mindset I often remind the beloved saints of Hope Alliance Bible Church to have, which is to believe there is always something more to be learned from familiar passages of Scripture, and more consistent application is always a worthy goal.

We live in a democratic society, and most of us enjoy the privilege of having a voice in governmental decisions and deciding who should rule over us and lead us. History teaches us that the most common form of governmental rule by far, however, is that of a king or queen. Some have been benevolent, while others dictatorial, but kings and kingdoms were around for thousands of years before the birth of Christ. Kings and kingdoms have incessantly battled one another for control of other people's lives for various reasons, some of which have been purely selfish. Our Lord Christ Jesus, eternally existent as God and later born in flesh to be King of the Jews and King over all, is the perfect fulfillment of what a King should be. The stories we will study in this book continue to teach us why we must learn to let the rightful King rule over everything we purpose to do as well as every aspect of our lives.

Many people refuse to acknowledge the existence of the King of kings and Lord of lords, Jesus the Christ. Others know of Him but seem to think He doesn't mind letting them try to run their own lives as the king or queen of their own kingdom. I trust as you read the following pages, you will glean fresh insights into how you can release your hold on your own little kingdom and get more involved in His kingdom, which is and is to come and will last forever.

This book first took shape as a preached series at my church. I only made introductory remarks on the first nine chapters of First Samuel, the focus of this book, as we began our study of First Samuel. I wanted to start when the narrative first had Saul come on the scene. From there, I did not attempt to do a verse-by-verse study, choosing instead to paint with broad strokes, so to speak, by looking at a few chapters every week and extracting key elements in those large sections.

My goal was not simply to do a historical study, but to help the listeners apply those historical lessons to modern life. Those men and their followers struggled with the same things we struggle with, and I wanted my congregation to see that, but then to have ammunition to fight the battle we all fight every day. We must decide whose kingdom we are going to serve: the Lord's or our own.

Jesus did not come preaching a doctrine of the Church. He came proclaiming the kingdom of God was at hand. Do a word search of church and kingdom in the gospels and you will find one reference to church (see Matthew 16), but multiple references to the kingdom of heaven or God. Jesus went on to teach what it meant to be a citizen of God's kingdom, starting with the Beatitudes in Matthew 5 and ending with His death on the cross. Well, it didn't really end there, for when Jesus came back from the dead, He continued to teach His disciples about the Kingdom and its implications for their lives.

The apostles carried on Jesus' work and that work was

to preach the kingdom of God. It became clear that there were many opponents to the Kingdom message, just as there had been in Jesus' ministry. There were doctrinal disputes and arguments, but the real issue was about the Kingdom and who was the rightful king. Paul continued that work as he traveled to Gentile lands, also proclaiming the kingdom of God under the authority of King Jesus. And the reaction to Paul's kingdom message was just as pronounced as it had been from the Jews.

The issue is still the same, for today people resist coming under the rule of a king, especially in our individualistic societies as I mentioned earlier. We want to decide for ourselves where our allegiance and obedience should lie. We want to say what we want, live with who we want in a way that we want, control our wealth and leisure time as we want, and maintain our image of God we want or prefer, all with interference from no one. In other words, we want to establish our own kingdom with our own rules and impose those rules as we see fit. We are the sovereign lord over every aspect of our own lives. We want to serve and maintain our kingdom.

Jesus addressed this dichotomy in His earliest teaching on prayer, when He taught us to pray "thy kingdom come, thy will be done" (Matthew 6:10). That was a simple description of our human dilemma; we had to choose which kingdom we would serve. King Saul faced it and "chose poorly," as the knight at the end of *Indiana Jones and the Last Crusade* said. King David chose wisely, most of the time, and it was the secret to his remarkable legacy that still exists today (we in the church sing his poetry and the modern nation of Israel still calls itself the people of David). Our legacy, yours and mine, will be determined by our own choice of which kingdom we will serve—our own or His.

I would urge you to read through First Samuel as you read through the book. I did not include all the text in this book, but rather chose some highlights and supplemented them with portions from other books of the Bible. I encourage you to journal your thoughts and insights as you read through this book and First Samuel. If you want to hear the preached version, you can go to our church website, listed at the end of this book, and hear my thoughts as well as read them.

The Kingdom is no less important or relevant today than

it was for David and Saul, and for Jesus, Paul, and the other apostles. The Kingdom is still what we preach and Kingdom principles are what we are discipled to live by. May this humble offering contribute something to your understanding of the Kingdom, but more importantly, may it help you become a better, more obedient, and fruitful citizen of the Kingdom.

Dr. Ron Morrison
Cleveland, Ohio
May 2019

FIRST SAMUEL 8-10

THE THRONE IS NO GAME

One of many impressive things about the Bible is the truth and transparency found in the stories. At no point did the authors, inspired by the Holy Spirit, attempt to hide the frailties and failures of God's people. Some of the failures were cataclysmic, and others were simply a matter of human weakness with minimal damage, but they are all included for the reason shared with us in Romans 15:4: "For whatever things were written before were written for our learning, that we through the patience and comfort of the Scriptures might have hope." We can take hope today because flawed people in the past not only served the Lord, but did great things for Him. If they did, we have hope to do so as well. As we begin our study, let's start with King Saul and look at his life in the account found in First Samuel chapters eight through ten.

I never assume readers or listeners are well acquainted with the Old Testament, so let's see where we are in history as we begin our study of First Samuel. You are familiar with the Genesis creation account of God speaking this world into existence and forming man from the dust of the earth and Eve from Adam's side.

Then the Fall of man came, bringing with it death and sin that eventually led to the flood in Noah's time through which eight human beings survived. Then there is the story of the Tower of Babel in Genesis 11, where people came together for all the wrong reasons. God had told them to scatter but they wanted to stay put, so God had to cause them to move on and fill the earth, using the confusion of different languages being spoken for the first time.

That led to a world full of people living in total absence of a relationship with the Lord, so He called Abraham from Ur of the Chaldees and led him to the Promised Land. There God promised He would create a nation from this man whose descendants would be more numerous than the stars in the sky and the sand on the seashore. The rest of Genesis (from chapter 12 to chapter 50) is about Abraham, his family, and the Hebrew people.

We meet Abraham, Isaac, Jacob, and Joseph and the book ends with Abraham's descendants living in Egypt to avoid a famine covering the earth.

When we get to Exodus, God has already said the people were going to be enslaved by the Egyptians. That came to pass, and the people were in captivity for more than 400 years until God raised up Moses to lead them out of Egypt back to Abraham's Promised Land. After Moses had 80 years of training, he was ready for his call to lead the people back. Let me repeat: Moses was called after 80 years of training. I know I want to retire after 80, but God said to Moses after those 80 years, "Now you're ready to do what I want." I emphasize that so you don't misunderstand however long God takes to train you. Your job is to be ready whenever He says it is time to go.

For the rest of Exodus, we read about the plagues, God's people coming out of Egypt, the miracles, the parting of the Red Sea, the giving of the Ten Commandments, and the building of the tabernacle for worship. The next book, Leviticus, is primarily a worship manual to teach the people how to worship a holy God.

The book of Numbers tells the story of the people going in to take the Promised Land until their disobedience caused a serious delay. The tribes sent twelve spies in to scout out the land so they would know what they needed to do to go in and take it. Ten of the scouts were intimidated by what they saw and the size of the opposition there. Only Joshua and Caleb came back with enough faith to say that with God it was possible to go in. The thinking of those two was, "God said we can do this, so we can do this. They do not stand a chance! He's with us. It doesn't matter how big they are. Look how big our God is!"

We know what happened when the majority ruled because the majority were ungodly. They disheartened the people and God's judgment for their disobedience was that the entire adult generation who did not believe and trust the Lord had to die in the Wilderness. After 40 years of wasted time, the Israelites were close to repeating the same mistake because the same unbelief their parents demonstrated began to manifest itself in the next generation. Moses became so frustrated that he struck a rock twice instead of speaking to it in the presence of God, thus losing his opportunity to go into the Promised Land. Then Joshua, the Hebrew word for Jesus, led the people in.

Moses introduced God's law to the people, representing what God required of the people—although it did not empower them to obey or follow it. God was always teaching symbolically, so Joshua (Jesus) led the people into the Promised Land. The Law showed them their need, but it took Jesus to get them into the Land. All throughout the book of Joshua, we read how the Israelites tried to conquer their enemies and settle the land, revealing a history of partial, sporadic obedience. When they trusted God, they would win. When they didn't trust God, they would lose.

Throughout the entire book of Judges, God raised up leaders in different parts of the country to lead His people as they settled the Land. We see a cycle of falling into sin, being taken captive by their enemies, crying out to God, and God raising up another judge to lead them to another victory. We see that cycle again and again in their history throughout Judges. Then we get to Samuel, who was the last of the great judges of Israel, and the people were getting tired. They didn't want a judge because Samuel's sons weren't godly like their father was—and that brings us to these chapters and the start of our study.

Even when parents are godly, there's no guarantee their kids will be godly. We have no record of Samuel doing anything wrong in his leadership career, but still his sons were not godly like he was. The people cried out again to God, but this time they asked for a king like the other nations had, a king who would lead them in battle. That's where we are when we get to First Samuel chapter 8.

By the way, I've worked to be able to present the history of the Old Testament as I just wrote it because it's important to commit it to memory. I want to be prepared to answer anyone who asks me the reason why any book in the Bible, especially the Old Testament, is important to me as a believer. I want to tell them its role in salvation history and its relevance to a person's walk with the Lord.

GOD'S KING

In 1 Samuel 8 the word of God says,

¹ Now it came to pass when Samuel was old that he

made his sons judges over Israel. [2] The name of his firstborn was Joel, and the name of his second, Abijah; they were judges in Beersheba. [3] But his sons did not walk in his ways; they turned aside after dishonest gain, took bribes, and perverted justice. [4] Then all the elders of Israel gathered together and came to Samuel at Ramah, [5] and said to him, "Look, you are old. Your sons do not walk in your ways. Now make us a king to judge us like all the nations" (1 Samuel 8:1-5).

Notice that they did not commend Samuel for doing a great job, but rather told him he was getting old!

We learned in Deuteronomy 17 that God intended the Hebrew nation to be a theocracy, which is a nation ruled by God (*theos* is the Greek word for God, and it is the root for our word theology). Israel was designated to be different. God was their King and ruler, but He did design them to be a monarchy with a visible, human king at some point. Like many of us, they went ahead of God's timing. We want what we want when we want it, and Israel wanted a king and they wanted one right then and there—no more waiting.

When we read Deuteronomy, we see that God had planned at some point in their history to give them a king:

[14] "When you come to the land which the Lord your God is giving you, and possess it and dwell in it, and say, 'I will set a king over me like all the nations that are around me,' [15] you shall surely set a king over you whom the Lord your God chooses; one from among your brethren you shall set as king over you; you may not set a foreigner over you, who is not your brother. [16] But he shall not multiply horses for himself, nor cause the people to return to Egypt to multiply horses, for the Lord has said to you, 'You shall not return that way again.' [17] Neither shall he multiply wives for himself, lest his heart turn away; nor shall he greatly multiply silver and gold for himself. [18] "Also it shall be, when he sits on the throne of his kingdom, that he shall write for himself a copy of this law in a book, from the one before the priests, the Levites. [19] And it shall be with

him, and he shall read it all the days of his life, that he may learn to fear the Lord his God and be careful to observe all the words of this law and these statutes, [20] that his heart may not be lifted above his brethren, that he may not turn aside from the commandment to the right hand or to the left, and that he may prolong his days in his kingdom, he and his children in the midst of Israel (Deuteronomy 17:14-20).

God predicted a few hundred years earlier what we read happening in 1 Samuel 8, that a day would come when the people would demand to have a king over them. God knew what was coming. There are people today who claim God doesn't know the future. I would have a problem worshiping a God who did not know the future. How would I know that he's going to keep me safe forever if he didn't know what was going to happen? I worship a God who can show me in the book of Revelation what's going to happen so I can trust Him as my Lord and Savior. I don't want a God who doesn't know what's going to happen tomorrow. I want one who knows and who can help me get through it!

In Deuteronomy 17, God stipulated the characteristics and behavior He wanted to see in His king. What did most of their kings do? They did almost all of what He told them *not* to do. They had too many wives. How many wives is too many? More than one is over the limit and Solomon was way over. He had one plus three zeros, or 1,000. That was three zeroes too many!

In verse 18, the Lord said if someone wanted to be the king, he was to write out his own personal copy of the first five books of the Bible. The king was to study it and put it in his heart. Did any of them do that? Some of them didn't even know where the Scriptures were.

I actually tried this once. I went to a computer and started to type out my own copy of the Bible. After I got through the first three or four chapters of Genesis, I thought, *This is going to take me too long.* Back then, the kings didn't even have typewriters or computers. The Lord wanted His kings to write out their own copy of the Scriptures. If they would sit down and write it, God knew some of it was going to find its way into their hearts.

Reading through the Bible is a big enough challenge, but to sit down and write out a copy would be a greater challenge.

A CRY FOR A KING

In 1 Samuel chapter 8, the people fulfilled God's prediction and cried out for a king. They were ahead of God's timing because the man God wanted to put on the throne wasn't ready yet. It becomes a problem when God lets us have it our way and then lets us regret that we got our way. We love to have it our way. A hamburger chain years ago promised that we could come in to their stores and have it our way. Frank Sinatra sang a song titled, *I Did It My Way.* Truth is, there are a lot of folks who went to hell because they did it their way. It's usually not good to brag that you did it your way, because your way is seldom God's way. We want to be our own king, but there is only one kingdom that is going to last, and that's the Kingdom of the Lord.

The people told Samuel, "We want a king." God told Samuel, "I know it stings but keep in mind, Samuel, they're not really rejecting you as much as they're rejecting Me." In the rest of chapter eight, God tells His people what their king is going to do to them, which was take advantage of and mistreat them.

When people and nations choose to reject God and His leadership, God gives them what they request along with the resulting consequences. That principle still applies today. The nation of Israel had the opportunity to be different than the other nations and have the blessings of God, but they had not learned the value of seeing the invisible things of God. They wanted what they could see and what they knew, and that meant they wanted a king.

Second Corinthians 5:7 states that "we walk by faith and not by sight." If all you can see is what you can see with your physical eyes, you can't see what you need to see. It's the invisible world that's going to last forever, and that's what you need to learn to see and focus on. You can only do that through the eyes of the Holy Spirit. In 1 Samuel 8, all they could see was that they didn't have a king riding out in front of them in battle like the other nations. They didn't and couldn't see that they were rejecting the Lord when they wanted a leader as a figurehead.

God was supposed to be their king and thus they were not to be like all the other nations. The reason they were or were not winning was not due to who was riding in front. It was the Lord who was (or wasn't) riding out front. God warned the people that ungodly leaders always had a selfish agenda. They take advantage of the people while making it look like they are serving them. It's like some of the modern prosperity preachers who make it appear they are serving others, but they are really serving themselves at someone else's expense.

Why is it that people are always sowing seed into their ministry and they're not sowing any into others? Why doesn't that work both ways? For example, if I give you 100 and I'm going to get 1,000, then why don't you give me 1,000, and you get 10,000? Am I missing something? Ungodly leaders always have an agenda. Will God bless you for giving? He will indeed. Is that your motive just to get more back than you give? Well then, that's a problem. That's a wonderful result, but if that ever becomes your reason for giving, you have a problem. The point is that ungodly leaders have an agenda and it's not God's agenda.

SAUL LOOKED GOOD

The Lord instructed Samuel to give the people what they wanted and in 1 Samuel 8:22, "Samuel said to the men of Israel, 'Every man go to a city.'" In 1 Samuel chapter 9:1, the word of God says, "There was a man of Benjamin whose name was Kish the son of Abiel, the son of Zeror, the son of Bechorath, the son of Aphiah, a Benjamite, and a mighty man of power."

Look at that heritage and family lineage. It's pointed out because Saul, his father, and his family came from good stock. They were well off and prosperous. They were noble, mighty, and valiant. "There was not a more handsome person than he [Saul] among the children of Israel. From his shoulders upward, he was taller than any of the people" (1 Samuel 9:2). Saul had it going on: He was tall, dark, and handsome. If anybody should be a leader, he looked the part. When we get to the story of David and Goliath, if the Philistines were sending their biggest man out to fight and Saul was the tallest man in Israel, shouldn't Saul have been the one going out to fight for Israel? Saul, however, wasn't stepping up or out. He became the king and leader, but he really didn't have what it took. He only looked like he did.

Examine your own heart to see whether you care more

about your own role and appearance or the kingdom of God. It's a blessing to look good on the outside. That's a gift of God but you're more blessed if you look good on the inside. It's a wonderful thing to have both, but as we will see later in 1 Samuel 16:7, "The Lord said to Samuel, 'Do not look at his appearance or at his physical stature, because I have refused him. For the Lord does not see as man sees; for man looks at the outward appearance, but the Lord looks at the heart.'"

We tend to look at what is outside, but God looks at the heart. First Peter 3:3-4 gives a classic example of the importance God places on the beauty of the inner person:

> Do not let your adornment be merely outward—arranging the hair, wearing gold, or putting on fine apparel, rather let it be the hidden person of the heart, with the incorruptible beauty of a gentle and quiet spirit, which is very precious in the sight of God.

God works through beauty and a person with a beautiful character can win people far more often than someone who is only beautiful on the outside. God created woman to provide beauty to mankind, for the glory of mankind is the woman. He warned in 1 Samuel 16, however, that if someone's beauty is only on the outside, that person is incomplete because God is looking at the heart. Saul looked good on the outside but he didn't look so good on the inside.

GOD USES CIRCUMSTANCES TO GUIDE US

First Samuel 9:3-6 states,

> [3] Now the donkeys of Kish, Saul's father, were lost. And Kish said to his son Saul, "Please take one of the servants with you, and arise, go and look for the donkeys." [4] So he passed through the mountains of Ephraim and through the land of Shalisha, but they did not find them. Then they passed through the land of Shaalim, and they were not there. Then he passed through the land of the Benjamites, but they did not find them. [5] When they had come to the land of Zuph, Saul said to his servant who was with him, "Come, let us return, lest my father cease caring about

the donkeys and become worried about us." [6] And he said to him, "Look now, there is in this city a man of God, and he is an honorable man; all that he says surely comes to pass. So let us go there; perhaps he can show us the way that we should go."

They were looking for some lost donkeys but could not find them. Saul said, "You know what? Dad's going to start worrying about me. Let's forget about these donkeys and go home," but his servant suggested they at least ask the man of God to see if he could help find them.

This seemed like a simple request and good idea, but God was in their idea and they didn't even realize it. We should be in awe of the sovereignty of God and notice how He uses what seems to be insignificant to lead us to divine appointments. Saul was going to run into his destiny even though he was only looking for some lost donkeys—or so he thought. He was going to meet Samuel the prophet, but not in church at worship.

Things that look insignificant to us can become significant when we realize God was (and is) behind them. A man named John Bunyan wrote a classic book, *Pilgrim's Progress*. Bunyan got drafted into military service and one day was supposed to go on guard duty except somebody wanted to trade duty times with him. Bunyan agreed and that somebody was killed that night. At that time, John Bunyan realized it should have been him and devoted the rest of his life to God.

I was in the U.S. Army from 1971-1973. While stationed in Germany I had an older gentleman as a roommate for a brief time. He had horrific nightmares and would wake up screaming and hollering. I found out in one of his sober moments that when he was in Vietnam, he was supposed to be the point man on patrol one day. They never have a platoon or group walk together because they don't want to risk everyone being taken out at the same time. My roommate made some feeble excuse and somebody else became the point man, and that point man was shot and killed. He was so guilt-ridden that the only way he could get through life was to get drunk every day. John Bunyan realized he should have been killed and he wound up giving his life wholeheartedly to the Lord while my roommate tried to drown his memories.

Ever heard of a man named William Cowper? He wrote a song most people think is a verse from the Bible. One of the famous lines is, "God works in mysterious ways." Cowper tried on five occasions to kill himself but whatever he tried just didn't work. He tried to fall on a knife. He tried hanging himself but somebody found him while he was passed out. He tried to drown himself and someone rescued him. Five times he tried to kill himself. He was so discouraged but he kept being rescued, so he wrote the song, *God Works in Mysterious Ways* and Cowper became a well-known servant of God.

SAUL MEETS SAMUEL

We must recognize God's sovereignty over events. God took Saul while he was out looking for donkeys and led him into his destiny. Saul was not there by accident and you're not where you are by accident. You're not where you are because you made right decisions along your path of life. God spared you because He has something for you. You don't know how many car accidents you've missed because of the sovereignty of God, and any one of them could have taken you out of here. You don't know who was out looking for you and God didn't let them find you because He had something else for you to do. Saul was getting ready to give up searching, but they heard there was a godly man around those parts who seemed to know what was going on. They decided to search him out:

> [7] Then Saul said to his servant, "But look, if we go, what shall we bring the man? For the bread in our vessels is all gone, and there is no present to bring to the man of God. What do we have? [8] And the servant answered Saul again and said, "Look, I have here at hand one-fourth of a shekel of silver. I will give that to the man of God, to tell us our way." [9] Formerly in Israel, when a man went to inquire of God, he spoke thus: "Come, let us go to the seer"; for he who is now called a prophet was formerly called a seer. [10] Then Saul said to his servant, "Well said; come, let us go." So they went to the city where the man of God was. [11] As they went up the hill to the city, they met some young women going out to draw water, and said to

them, "Is the seer here?" [12] And they answered them and said, "Yes, there he is, just ahead of you. Hurry now; for today he came to this city, because there is a sacrifice of the people today on the high place. [13] As soon as you come into the city, you will surely find him before he goes up to the high place to eat. For the people will not eat until he comes, because he must bless the sacrifice; afterward those who are invited will eat. Now therefore, go up, for about this time you will find him." [14] So they went up to the city. As they were coming into the city, there was Samuel, coming out toward them on his way up to the high place. [15] Now the Lord had told Samuel in his ear the day before Saul came, saying, [16] "Tomorrow about this time I will send you a man from the land of Benjamin, and you shall anoint him commander over My people Israel, that he may save My people from the hand of the Philistines; for I have looked upon My people, because their cry has come to Me." [17] So when Samuel saw Saul, the Lord said to him, "There he is, the man of whom I spoke to you. This one shall reign over my people." Let me just interject here that sadly reign in this context means to rule harshly. [18] Then Saul drew near to Samuel in the gate, and said, "Please tell me, where is the seer's house?" [19] Samuel answered Saul and said, "I am the seer. Go up before me to the high place, for you shall eat with me today; and tomorrow I will let you go and will tell you all that is in your heart. [20] But as for your donkeys that were lost three days ago, do not be anxious about them, for they have been found. And on whom is all the desire of Israel? Is it not on you and on all your father's house?" (1 Samuel 9:7-20).

Saul looked impressive, but he seemed to be lackadaisical where the things of the Lord were concerned. Samuel was the most famous judge in Israel and everybody knew about him, yet Saul was clueless about the man and had no idea where he lived. How is it that everybody in Israel knew about Samuel and Saul was clueless? Also, many of Israel's leaders were shepherds of lost sheep, but Saul was looking for some lost donkeys. Donkeys are not all that fast, so one would think there would be an easy-to-follow trail, but Saul never found them. His shepherding skills were lacking, and he never asked the Spirit of God to guide him. The servant of Saul was the one who suggested they go ask the man of God. Saul didn't even know there was a man of God nearby. Then Saul thought he had to pay Samuel to get information from him.

Both of Samuel's sons took advantage of those who came to them for religious services, and sadly some preachers today choose to "fleece the flock" rather than feed the flock of God. It shouldn't cost anything to find out what the "thus saith the Lord" is for your life. Samuel said he had been looking for Saul because God told him to appoint Saul king of Israel, and assured Saul his donkeys were on their way back home. God used lost donkeys to get Saul to his destiny, which speaks again to the truth that there are no coincidences in life.

What appears to be humility and shyness on Saul's part might really be a reluctance to serve God's kingdom instead of his own. Right after Samuel tells Saul that he was the desire of Israel, Saul says, "Aren't I a Benjamite of the smallest of the tribe of Israel? My family is the least of all the tribes in the nation of Israel. Why are you speaking to me like this?" Nothing he said made it sound like his family was all that significant, which left him incredulous that he would even be considered for the position. God had chosen Saul to become the leader of Israel, however, because that's what the people wanted.

In chapter 10, Samuel took a flask of oil and poured it on Saul's head, kissed him, and said,

> [1] "Is it not because the Lord has anointed you commander over His inheritance? [2] When you have departed from me today, you will find two men by Rachel's tomb in the territory of Benjamin at Zelzah; and they will say to you, 'The donkeys which you went to look for have been found. [3] And now your father has ceased caring about the donkeys and is worrying about you, saying, "What shall I do about my son?" (1 Samuel 10:1-3).

He went on to give Saul some signs to confirm what God was doing for him. Then he anointed him and said, "You're going to run into some men, this is going to happen, and you're going to prophesy." He was trying to give Saul every bit of confirmation he could that God's choice of him for king was true. When we read chapter 10, we see all those things Samuel said came to pass. The Bible reports that after he had this encounter with the Lord, God changed his heart: "So it was, when he had turned his back to go from Samuel, that God gave him another heart; and all those signs came to pass that day" (1 Samuel 10:9).

The question is: Exactly what happened in Saul's heart because nothing in Saul's life makes it look like he was ever a true worshiper? God changed and equipped him to do what he needed to do as a leader. That didn't necessarily make it a conversion experience because we don't find anything in Saul's life to give us confidence he truly loved and worshiped the Lord. God changed him to do what he wanted him to do.

Many times in the Old Testament, God empowered people to perform a service. In the New Testament when someone was born again, the Spirit of God would come to permanently indwell that person. In the Old Testament, God would come upon someone to get something done, but some of those people would not embrace him as Lord and Savior. Saul got equipped to do what he was called to do, but he didn't worship the Lord like he should have.

RELUCTANT SAUL

When Saul got back home after being gone for so long, he was probably asked about his trip. We read in 1 Samuel 10,

> [17] Then Samuel called the people together to the Lord at Mizpah, [18] and said to the children of Israel, "Thus says the Lord God of Israel: 'I brought up Israel out of Egypt, and delivered you from the hand of the Egyptians and from the hand of all kingdoms and from those who oppressed you.' [19] But you have today rejected your God, who Himself saved you from all your adversities and your tribulations; and you have said to Him, 'No, set a king over us!' Now therefore, present yourselves before the Lord by your tribes and by your

clans." [20] And when Samuel had caused all the tribes of Israel to come near, the tribe of Benjamin was chosen. [21] When he had caused the tribe of Benjamin to come near by their families, the family of Matri was chosen. And Saul the son of Kish was chosen. But when they sought him, he could not be found. [22] Therefore they inquired of the Lord further, "Has the man come here yet?" And the Lord answered, "There he is, hidden among the equipment" (1 Samuel 10:17–22).

Saul has already been anointed and told what he was going to do. Then came the celebration and coronation day when God revealed and confirmed publicly who he had chosen, eliminating other tribes so they all eventually realized it was Saul. Saul was supposed to walk out on stage for the coronation, but where was he? He was hiding. When it was time for Saul to be presented and anointed as king over Israel, he tried to hide among the baggage. Humility should accompany obedience, but it should never keep us from stepping up when we are called.

Some commentators interpret this to mean Saul was humble. But I have another interpretation. He was disobedient. Humility or shyness, if that's really what it was, is never an excuse for disobedience. Despite all that Saul had seen and heard, he didn't want to do what God had assigned him to do. It was an imposition and not consistent with Saul's ultimate life philosophy of "my kingdom come." This is what God wanted to happen but Saul was perhaps thinking, *I didn't go out looking to be king. I went out looking for some donkeys. I don't know if I have time to be the king of Israel for a God I really don't know that well. This is going to change my whole life and interrupt my schedule.*

Maybe you don't step up and do what God wants you to do because it's going to disrupt your life routine and schedule. It's not something you really want to do. It's all about your kingdom. You nominated yourself, voted for yourself, and ran unopposed every election to stay in your position as head of your kingdom. God is saying it is time for His kingdom to come.

Since you were a little child, you have been praying, "Thy kingdom come, thy will be done." Now it's time for you to be a part of that and you are not stepping up to the plate. Saul didn't want to do what God called him to do, so God had to say in front of everybody that he was hiding with the equipment. The biggest, tallest man in Israel was hiding himself among the equipment when God called him to work. That's pitiful! The people went to find him and brought him to stand before the assembly where he was indeed head-and-shoulders taller than any of the people. Samuel said to all the people, "Do you see him whom the Lord has chosen, that there is no one like him among all the people?"

> [24] All the people shouted and said, "Long live the king!" [25] Then Samuel explained to the people the behavior of royalty, and wrote it in a book and laid it up before the Lord. And Samuel sent all the people away, every man to his house. [26] And Saul also went home to Gibeah; and valiant men went with him, whose hearts God had touched. [27] But some rebels said, "How can this man save us?" So they despised him, and brought him no presents. But he held his peace (1 Samuel 10:24-27).

When Saul first got back after looking for the donkeys, his father asked what had happened on his trip. Saul never mentioned the encounter with Samuel or what Samuel had told him about being the king. We have to wonder why he didn't say anything about such a life-changing conversation. I don't understand that, but I have to conclude that he really didn't want to do what God called him to do.

Can you imagine going home after God had said you're going to be the next president or the pastor of the largest church in the country, and then you didn't even tell the people closest to you? You could at least tell them so they could pray for you, but Saul chose not to tell anyone.

God can and does use people to bring Him glory even when their desires are not in alignment with His will. Some people are good examples of what *not* to do. We all want to be used for His glory. God got glory out of Pharaoh, and it wasn't because Pharaoh wanted to do His will. I don't want to live my life as just a bad example, I want people to use my name in a positive way and not say, "Whatever you do, don't be like him. You don't want to go out like that, do you? However, if you don't stop doing things your way and begin doing things His way, you are in danger of missing your purpose and God's will for your life." Instead of singing, "Praise Him, praise Him, praise to the King of kings and Lord of lords," you'll be singing *I Did It My Way*. You're going to wind up in a place where no one sings or experiences any joy.

Choose wisely who you want to be king of your life because there's only one King who has eternal blessings for His subjects. The throne of your life is not a game to be approached lightly or casually. Who sits on that throne determines how effective you will be for Him and how fulfilled you will be as you look over your life at the end. Surrender joyfully to His will and don't be found hiding among the baggage of your life.

> *Lord, we pray that we would learn from the example of King Saul of how important it is to set our hearts in pursuit of Yours, and not treat Your will as a game or something we do not want to be bothered with. We recognize we have the same potential in us to fail miserably in spite of what You give us if we do not love You more than our own stuff and agendas. Continue to remind us that outward appearances and the accolades of others are meaningless in light of eternity, and only what is done for Christ will last. Help us distinguish between appearances of shyness and false humility, which can easily be hidden forms of pride and resistance to submit to Your will. May Your Spirit lead us to surrender and glorious service for our King Jesus. Amen.*

FROM MY KINGDOM TO THY KINGDOM

It's difficult for us to step down from the thrones of our lives. We want to run our own show and just call God along for the ride, for a bailout, or for needed resources. Life is a not a game in which we try to outsmart other people or figure out how we can get ahead. It's not about building our kingdom but about His kingdom. He is Lord of all, whether we acknowledge it or not. Better to do it when we are alive and can receive the gift of eternal life, rather than do it in forced submission and acknowledgment when it is too late to change our destiny.

The Scripture says every knee shall bow every tongue shall confess that Jesus is Lord, to the glory of God (see Isaiah 45:23 and Romans 14:11). The wise thing to do is to get off the throne of your own kingdom and acknowledge Him as Lord, then find out why He has placed you on earth to live the life He's designed for you to live.

This book focuses on the lives of the first kings of Israel to learn what they did right and what they did wrong in regard to God's kingdom. The first man up is King Saul, as we saw in the first chapter, and it's sad to say that much of Saul's life serves as a bad example for us. When we study Saul, nine out of the ten things we find are things we don't want to emulate. He was a man who was given every opportunity to succeed. Despite all that, he failed miserably.

Who we think we are and how we view God will quickly show up in our choices and behavior. As we study the life of Saul, we discover that his view of God was distorted. He thought a lot about himself while he thought too little about the Lord. He had power, but he thought that power could be manipulated whenever he needed it to serve his own purposes. Does it sound like anybody you know?

We learned in the first chapter that Israel wanted a king,

which was not a bad decision but did involve bad timing. God had already said that eventually He would give them a king, but they got ahead of God. Have you ever done that? Samuel was given the responsibility to anoint Saul, the people's choice. He looked like a leader since he was head and shoulders above everybody else. He had it going on the outside but sadly not on the inside.

Let's review our first glimpse of Saul again. Samuel met Saul because Saul was looking for some lost donkeys and had spent a few days trying to find them. By the sovereign decree of God, Saul bumped into Samuel. God had already told Samuel he was the one that God was going to anoint as king, so Samuel invited Saul to stay with him. He served him dinner and they spent some time together while Samuel let him know he was God's chosen man for the hour. Saul was amazed and incredulous. How can it be me, he asked? Now let's go back and look at 1 Samuel chapter 10:

> [14] Then Saul's uncle said to him and his servant, "Where did you go?" So he said, "To look for the donkeys. When we saw that *they were* nowhere *to be found,* we went to Samuel." [15] And Saul's uncle said, "Tell me, please, what Samuel said to you." [16] So Saul said to his uncle, "He told us plainly that the donkeys had been found." But about the matter of the kingdom, he did not tell him what Samuel had said (1 Samuel 10:14-16).

The Holy Spirit never filled up space in a book of the Bible for no reason. He wants us to take notice that Saul didn't care to talk about what was much more important than finding donkeys. For whatever reason, he kept the most important information he had ever received to himself. Then on coronation day, when he was anointed, where was he? We learned in the last chapter that he was hiding among the baggage. He was not humble; he was disobedient. He was supposed to step up to the plate because God had called him. I don't care how shy anyone is; whenever God tells us to do something, you stand up, go forward, and do it. Humility is never an excuse for disobedience.

Let's move on to 1 Samuel 11. Even if we don't understand

or agree with the leaders God chooses, we are obligated to pray for them. Let me modernize that language. It doesn't matter who you voted for or the winner's party affiliation. God says pray for all those who are in authority. Whether you like them or not, whether you agree with them or not, you're responsible as a Kingdom citizen to pray so that God will give them wisdom because they're in a position of authority—and they will need lots of wisdom. The same holds true for politicians and church leaders.

When you read through these next few chapters, or whenever you read any of the Old Testament, it helps if you have a map in front of you because you can get lost in some of the conversations. If you don't see where the cities are and study the geography in the narrative, you won't have a complete understanding of the story. If someone is in a valley, in the mountains, on the plains, or has a river to cross, it adds to the drama of what's going on when you see where they were. That's why it would be helpful to read through these sections with a map in front of you.

SAUL PRESSED INTO ACTION

In chapter 11, there was a horrific situation where some of the men of Gilead were being threatened and intimidated. The story tells us that Nahash, the Ammonite head, encamped against them, and so the people of Jabesh Gilead made an appeal to Nahash, saying, "Can you make a covenant with us and we will serve you?" By the way, Nahash was an Ammonite and the Ammonites come from Lot's incestuous relationship with one of his daughters.

The covenant conditions Nabash proposed were that the Ammonites would gouge out the right eye of every man in Gilead. I can't imagine that, but back then, there were no rules of war. They asked for seven days to think it over, agreeing that if they did not come up with a better solution, they would submit. These people were God's people, the same God who promised that if they obeyed Him, He would give them victory over their enemies. Because they would not obey God, they are being forced into submission.

What is the application for us today? The rules of engagement haven't changed. If we serve God, He will watch over and protect us. If we refuse, then we will suffer the consequences. How often have we submitted to horrific spiritual, demonic subjugation because we refused to obey God? God promises victory if we obey Him, but hard times if we do not.

For those seven days, the people wept and mourned. The word of their dilemma got to Saul, the new king. God empowered Saul and he went out to lead the people of God to victory. The Scripture tells us that Saul cut up an ox and sent it to the different peoples of Israel, promising the same would happen to them if they didn't rally and help Saul and his army fight. By doing that, Saul assembled more than 300,000 soldiers, and God gave them victory. For one of the few times in his life, Saul did something right. We read in 1 Samuel 11:12-15,

> [12] Then the people said to Samuel, "Who is he who said, 'Shall Saul reign over us?' Bring the men, that we may put them to death." [13] But Saul said, "Not a man shall be put to death this day, for today the Lord has accomplished salvation in Israel." [14] Then Samuel said to the people, "Come, let us go to Gilgal and renew the kingdom there." [15] So all the people went to Gilgal, and there they made Saul king before the Lord in Gilgal. There they made sacrifices of peace offerings before the Lord, and there Saul and all the men of Israel rejoiced greatly.

In 1 Samuel 10:27, we read, "But some rebels said, 'How can this man [Saul] save us?' So they despised him, and brought him no presents. But he held his peace.'"

When Saul led them to victory, the people wanted to know where those men were who didn't want to accept Saul's leadership because they wanted to kill them! Saul didn't allow that to happen, however, saying God had brought them a great victory, suggesting they should give God thanks instead. Saul was a popular choice, but he wasn't a unanimous choice. God empowered him to lead the Israelites to victory, and he wisely forgave his opposition.

Do you need to show more grace to some of your critics who said you'll never amount to much? When you succeed, do you want to get even? How do you treat the people who once criticized you—people who didn't vote for you or whatever it was that you wanted to do? Can you look back on your life and say, "You didn't agree with me then, but let's lock arms and walk together now. We're on the same team."

If you are a Christian and your brother and sister are Christians, in spite of your differences, you are on the same team and in the same army. It's not the time to be fighting your fellow soldiers. In fact, there is never a good time for fellow soldiers to be killing one another when the enemy is the real problem. Even Saul said there is a time to let it go.

When Saul later started making other terrible and bizarre decisions, we are going to ask if this is the same man who acted so nobly and graciously in this event. He didn't seem to have everything connected properly in his brain. In this instance, he got it right. Good leaders remind us of the blessings of obedience and consequences of disobedience. Regardless of what they do, however, we must remember that we are sinning if we refuse to pray for those who are in authority over us.

CONSEQUENCES

As we move into 1 Samuel 12, Samuel emerges to remind the people of what their God had done to allow them to be in a position where they could go forth in victory if they chose to do so. He reminded them of their history that every time they disobeyed, they got a beat down. It's a simple fact of life that there are consequences to your choices. You do it God's way, you walk in victory. If you don't do it God's way, you will pay a price.

Why does God allow consequences? It's because consequences are wonderful teaching tools even though they are unpleasant. They keep us from repeatedly doing the same wrong thing and getting hurt. That's why little children have parents who discipline them in love. Even before they can understand complicated subjects, they understand painful consequences when they disobey Mommy's or Daddy's voice. They can learn obedience before they learn to speak. If parents do it right when their children are little, they don't have to fight them when they are grown and 35 years old.

It's not referred to as abuse, but rather is called discipline for a reason. That child cannot reason with parents when they are two or three years old. It may take one moment of putting the fear of God in the child that may last for the rest of their lives. My father used to brag that the reason I don't recall any spankings is because I got all mine before I was old enough to remember. Something got instilled in my little brain early on that things go well whenever I obeyed my parents.

My sister and brother have told me about some of my spankings because they are a bit older than I. For some reason, they delight in telling me about those times, but I have no conscious memory of ever getting a spanking. Therefore, in my mind, I was a wonderful child. They have a slightly different understanding of the story. The point is this: Consequences help us learn to obey the Lord. We read in 1 Samuel 12:10-16:

> [10] Then they cried out to the Lord, and said, 'We have sinned, because we have forsaken the Lord and served the Baals and Ashtoreths; but now deliver us from the hand of our enemies, and we will serve You.' [11] And the Lord sent Jerubbaal, Bedan, Jephthah, and Samuel, and delivered you out of the hand of your enemies on every side; and you dwelt in safety. [12] And when you saw that Nahash king of the Ammonites came against you, you said to me, 'No, but a king shall reign over us,' when the Lord your God was your king. [13] "Now therefore, here is the king whom you have chosen and whom you have desired. And take note, the Lord has set a king over you. [14] If you fear the Lord and serve Him and obey His voice, and do not rebel against the commandment of the Lord, then both you and the king who reigns over you will continue following the Lord your God. [15] However, if you do not obey the voice of the Lord, but rebel against the commandment of the Lord, then the hand of the Lord will be against you, as it was against your fathers. [16] "Now therefore, stand and see this great thing which the Lord will do before your eyes."

This passage informs us that Saul was not God's ideal choice. God anointed and allowed him to be king and promised if he did what God told him, He would allow Saul to be successful and victorious. Saul refused. Why are we so slow to learn our lessons? It's not that complicated and requires a simple act of obedience. The people still didn't grasp it either. In 1 Samuel 11:17, we read,

> "Is today not the wheat harvest? I will call to the Lord, and He will send thunder and rain, that you may perceive and see that your wickedness is great, which you have done in the sight of the Lord, in asking a king for yourselves." So Samuel called and the Lord sent thunder and rain that day and all the people greatly feared the Lord and Samuel.

In an urban environment, we can read this passage and not understand its significance. In an agricultural society, there's a window of opportunity for the harvest. It's the season when it's not supposed to rain but Samuel in essence said, "Just so you can see that God is displeased, I'm going to call on the Lord to change the weather. Does that impress you?"

There are other instances where God intervened in nature's natural processes, which He established to show His power and control over His creation. Elijah called down fire from heaven (see 1 Kings 17) and God stopped the sun when Joshua was fighting (see Joshua 10). We have a God who can do what He wants to do. In this case, there was thunder and a deluge, so much that they could not harvest. This was not ordinary thunder and rain but like the kind that occurred during the plagues in Egypt. This was frightening and life-threatening. If it had not stopped, all that wheat they thought they were going to harvest to eat and make money on was going to be lost.

The people's response is recorded in 1 Samuel 12:19, "And all the people said to Samuel, 'Pray for your servants to the Lord your God, that we may not die; for we have added to all our sins the evil of asking a king for ourselves.'" They knew they had erred and asked Samuel to pray for them. They didn't want God to destroy them because it had not been God's will when they asked for a king. Samuel was a gracious man and godly leader as evidenced by his response:

> 20 Then Samuel said to the people, "Do not fear. You have done all this wickedness; yet do not turn aside

from following the Lord, but serve the Lord with all your heart. [21] And do not turn aside; for then you would go after empty things which cannot profit or deliver, for they are nothing. [22] For the Lord will not forsake His people, for His great name's sake, because it has pleased the Lord to make you His people. [23] Moreover, as for me, far be it from me that I should sin against the Lord in ceasing to pray for you; but I will teach you the good and the right way. [24] Only fear the Lord, and serve Him in truth with all your heart; for consider what great things He has done for you. [25] But if you still do wickedly, you shall be swept away, both you and your king" (1 Samuel 12:20-25).

Samuel said it would be a sin if he didn't pray for them. He made one thing clear, and that was the people needed to keep doing what God wanted them to do or else they and their king would be swept away.

The busyness of pastoral ministry today has contributed to a sinful neglect of a primary responsibility that aligns with what Samuel declared to the Israelites in the aforementioned passage. The precedent of leaders spending time in prayer for others was declared in Acts 6, where the apostles oversaw the process of selecting other Spirit-filled leaders to minister to important needs so prayer, preaching, and teaching were not neglected.

It grieves me when believers only pray for leaders who are members of their same political party, rather than follow the instructions clearly given in Scripture:

[1] Therefore I exhort first of all that supplications, prayers, intercessions, and giving of thanks be made for all men, [2] for kings and all who are in authority, that we may lead a quiet and peaceable life in all godliness and reverence. [3] For this is good and acceptable in the sight of God our Savior, [4] who desires all men to be saved and to come to the knowledge of the truth (1 Timothy 2:1-4).

I find more people criticizing and complaining about their leaders than praying for them. If we did more praying and less criticizing of our leaders, some things might change, but it's easier to criticize than to pray for someone. Maybe we should make a rule that we are not going to criticize anybody until we first pray for them.

The Lord allows us to be put to the test so we will learn if we are serious about obeying his word. Notice I did not say so He can learn if we're serious about obeying His word, for He already knows. He's going to put you to the test so *you* can learn if you are serious about obeying the Lord, or just doing it when things are going well.

UNDERESTIMATING THE ENEMY

When we arrive at 1 Samuel 13:1, we see that Saul has been ruling for a few years. Verse two reported that Saul chose for himself three thousand men of Israel; two thousand were assigned to Saul at Michmash and in the mountains of Bethel, and a thousand were with Jonathan in Gibeah of Benjamin. The rest of the people he sent away, every man to his tent.

Saul had access to hundreds of thousands of soldiers, but he chose this standing bodyguard group of 3,000 soldiers because that's all he felt he needed for the situation. He divided his forces and sent Jonathan to attack the Philistines. If you look on a map, you will see that the Philistines lived close to the Mediterranean Sea. They were a constant threat to the people of God.

> ³ And Jonathan attacked the garrison of the Philistines that was in Geba, and the Philistines heard of it. Then Saul blew the trumpet throughout all the land, saying, "Let the Hebrews hear!" ⁴ Now all Israel heard it said that Saul had attacked a garrison of the Philistines, and that Israel had also become an abomination to the Philistines. And the people were called together to Saul at Gilgal (1 Samuel 13:2-4).

The sound of the trumpet would call the people to battle because they didn't have CNN or the internet to notify everyone and spread the news as we do today. They had to blow the trumpet so the word would be communicated from valley to valley and from home to home: It was time to assemble for battle. The sound of the trumpet always meant something. When the church is raptured (see 1 Thessalonians 4:13-18), the Bible tells us we will hear the sound of the trumpet just like when Saul called his army together. It will be God calling us home.

The Israelites were gathering together for battle but there was a problem. Look at 1 Samuel 13:5 and remember that Saul only had a few thousand men:

> [5] Then the Philistines gathered together to fight with Israel, thirty thousand chariots and six thousand horsemen, and people as the sand which is on the seashore in multitude. And they came up and encamped in Michmash, to the east of Beth Aven. [6] When the men of Israel saw that they were in danger (for the people were distressed), then the people hid in caves, in thickets, in rocks, in holes, and in pits. [7] And some of the Hebrews crossed over the Jordan to the land of Gad and Gilead.
>
> As for Saul, he was still in Gilgal, and all the people followed him trembling. [8] Then he waited seven days, according to the time set by Samuel. But Samuel did not come to Gilgal; and the people were scattered from him. [9] So Saul said, "Bring a burnt offering and peace offerings here to me." And he offered the burnt offering. [10] Now it happened, as soon as he had finished presenting the burnt offering, that Samuel came; and Saul went out to meet him, that he might greet him. [11] And Samuel said, "What have you done? "Saul said, "When I saw that the people were scattered from me, and that you did not come within the days appointed, and that the Philistines gathered together at Michmash, [12] then I said, 'The Philistines will now come down on me at Gilgal, and I have not made supplication to the Lord.' Therefore I felt compelled, and offered a burnt offering" (1 Samuel 13:5-12).

When they started this battle, they saw enemy soldiers that looked like the grains of sand on the seashore while they had only a few thousand soldiers. You don't have to be a mathematical genius to figure out that they were hopelessly outnumbered and the situation did not look good. They needed some big-time help. What should a believer do when he or she is outnumbered? Pray? Pray harder?

Open Our Eyes, Lord

Let's look at a classic example of what someone did who was outnumbered in 2 Kings 6. We spend most of our lives not seeing what God really wants us to see. Young people think they have another 60 years of life and opportunities, but God doesn't promise that to anybody. Today could be their last day to respond to Christ—and it could be yours too. I often wonder if people could get a one-second glimpse of hell or a one-second glimpse of glory, would they live differently?

We don't see what we need to see because we don't let God show us. Did you ever try to point out something to someone but they are so arrogant, they don't even want to look? At some point, you stop arguing with the blind man about the color of the rainbow because you realize people just want to argue about something they can't possibly see or know. Second Kings tells us,

> 8 Now the king of Syria was making war against Israel; and he consulted with his servants, saying, "My camp will be in such and such a place." 9 And the man of God sent to the king of Israel, saying, "Beware that you do not pass this place, for the Syrians are coming down there." 10 Then the king of Israel sent someone to the place of which the man of God had told him. Thus he warned him, and he was watchful there, not just once or twice. 11 Therefore the heart of the king of Syria was greatly troubled by this thing; and he called his servants and said to them, "Will you not show me which of us is for the king of Israel?" 12 And one of his servants said, "None, my lord, O king; but Elisha, the prophet who is in Israel, tells the king of Israel the words that you speak in your bedroom" (2 Kings 6:8-12).

God doesn't need hidden cameras or microphones to find out what's going on. He knows what everybody is saying, thinking, and doing without any of that. In case you had not noticed, He can tell you if you really need and want to know. That's what he was doing in this instance for this king.

13 So he said, "Go and see where he is, that I may send

and get him." And it was told him, saying, "Surely he is in Dothan." ¹⁴ Therefore he sent horses and chariots and a great army there, and they came by night and surrounded the city. ¹⁵ And when the servant of the man of God arose early and went out, there was an army, surrounding the city with horses and chariots. And his servant said to him, "Alas, my master! What shall we do?" ¹⁶ So he answered, "Do not fear, for those who are with us are more than those who are with them" (2 Kings 6:13-16).

Elisha's servant said, "Wait a minute. I'm looking out and I see thousands of soldiers and I see two of us." Elisha responded, "Don't worry, we have them outnumbered," causing the servant to wonder, *Is this some new math, Elisha?*

¹⁷ Elisha prayed Lord I pray open his eyes that he may see. Then the Lord opened the eyes of the young man, and he saw. And behold, the mountain was full of horses and chariots of fire all around Elisha. ¹⁸ So when the Syrians came down to him, Elisha prayed to the Lord, and said, "Strike this people, I pray, with blindness." And He struck them with blindness according to the word of Elisha (2 Kings 6:17-18).

The Lord struck the enemies of Israel with blindness, making them helpless and easy to be captured. Isn't it comforting to know our Lord can easily defeat our enemies?

Some of you have never read the Old Testament so you don't know what you have going for you in your favor. These same angels are not going anywhere. They still surround and protect the people of God. Just because you feel like you're outnumbered or it looks like you're outnumbered, isn't the case. The problem is you don't see what the Lord wants you to see. We need to say, "Lord, open my eyes so I can see what you have around me to protect me to do Your will." Saul hadn't grown enough to see the invisible, the power of God, or the resources of God that are available. Therefore, Saul panicked.

We often appear to be outnumbered by the enemy. Mature believers must help weaker believers move from fear to faith when we listen to the news media today. As born-again

Christians, we are in the minority in our country. It would be easy to conclude that we might as well give up because what we believe is not going to be embraced or received by the masses. The enemy may be whispering in your spirit that you may as well compromise and go along with all this foolishness. Don't listen to him.

God and His word are always right; they will not change. It does not matter if you are one against a million. If you know what the word of God says, then stand on it because if you don't, those people in that crowd are not going to hear the Word if you don't share it. That's why Jesus said we are salt and light in this dying world.

OBEY THE LORD

Saul had been given some detailed instructions. They seemed difficult and nonsensical to him in relation to the situation he was facing. The instructions to him, however, were clear: Wait seven days and then Samuel would be there to perform the offerings and the sacrifice. It's never a good choice to disobey a clear command from the Lord. He is always on time and we would do well to wait for Him. What good does it do to get ahead of God's perfect timing? As one old preacher used to say, "If you get ahead of God, what are you going to do when you get there?"

Saul was to wait seven days until Samuel arrived. Then Saul would find out what God wanted him to do and see. The problem is described in verse six, for the men of Israel saw they were in danger. They started hiding in the thickets and caves, in the rocks and holes. They were so outnumbered that they were looking for any place to hide so they would not get hurt or killed. The people who followed Saul were shaking and trembling with fear. We read in 1 Samuel 13:8, "Then he waited seven days, according to the time set by Samuel. But Samuel did not come to Gilgal; and the people were scattered from him."

Put yourself in Saul shoes. He was the leader. He looked around and every day his army was getting smaller so he felt like he had to do *something*. What was he told to do? He was told to wait, but the people were leaving. He felt he had to do something because God was taking too long. Have you ever been there?

God is taking too long and you have to do something. You come up with ten possible solutions, none of which are what God told you to do. The test from the Lord was to show what Saul had been covering up. We see the reason God didn't want to put him on the throne was that he didn't trust God or have adequate faith.

Young people, try to wait on the Lord when your friends are pressuring you, saying, "Look what you're missing out on. Why are you trying to stay pure and missing out on the easy money by selling drugs? What are you waiting for?" Your response should be, "I want a future and a life, and God told me not to do any of that."

If you do what peer pressure tries to force you to do, you will miss out on a lot of what the Lord wants you to experience as you grow closer to him. Yielding to peer pressure will bring a lot of pain, hurt, agony, and sorrow, after the passing pleasures of sin are history. We want you to experience the joy that only comes from serving the Lord.

Financial investments often take a long time to mature and develop, but they're worth it. The same is true for a garden. No one plants one day and sees a harvest the next day. God wants us to plant seeds of obedience and watch the fruit come from it—in due season. Satan gets many of our young people to sin because it pays off in immediate pleasure, but it can lead to a lifetime of painful consequences. At the moment, it may feel good to sin, and that's why people do it so readily. Holiness doesn't pay off right away, or at least it doesn't seem like it. It is far better to choose a life of holiness, however, so you will not have to face a future of regret.

Some preachers give up preaching the word of God because a lot of people want something else. The only thing God gave us to preach is His word. The only thing that will ever grow healthy disciples is His word. When we preach it, the fruit will remain throughout all eternity. Some people don't have the courage to do what God wants them to do, so they choose to manipulate or preach the prosperity gospel. "Do this and God will make you rich by this time next month or next year."

Pastors have to decide if they are going to teach people how to give or sell chicken dinners to raise money? You may be tempted to think, *Why should I get a job whenever I can just play the lottery and get rich tomorrow or just sell some drugs and get rich tonight? Maybe I'll die tomorrow.* Saul was tempted with the thought, *Are you going to wait on the Lord, or are you going to find a solution* like so many of us? If Saul had chosen to follow God's kingdom and surrender his life and leadership, he would have waited. If you choose God's kingdom, you should wait too.

In 1 Samuel 13:9, we learn that Samuel felt like he had waited long enough. It was day seven and Samuel was nowhere to be found. Saul decided to go ahead and offer the sacrifice. He was sure God would overlook this slight adjustment in plans, and Saul was counting on God doing what He always does—which is be gracious. Don't we do that? Don't we think that if we just go to church and tithe, we will get everything we want? If our hearts aren't right, it doesn't matter what else we do.

When we do wrong, it's better to confess and repent rather than try to justify our actions. God already knows the real reasons. They usually include a lack of faith and trust. Saul offered a burnt offering and he felt then God was going to come through for him. The language is interesting in 1 Samuel 13:10: "Now it happened, as soon as he had finished presenting the burnt offering, that Samuel came."

Day seven hadn't finished, but Saul couldn't wait any longer. It's sad that Saul was clueless here, for he thought Samuel would be happy to see him, and delighted that Saul had taken the initiative to proceed with the sacrifice. That was not the case, however, for Samuel said, "What have you done?" (1 Samuel 13:11).

Look through Scriptures and see how often questions are asked whenever someone has messed up. After he had murdered his brother, Abel, the Lord asked Cain, "What have you done? Where's your brother?" Cain's lying and heartless response could be summarized by saying "I don't know. Wasn't my day to watch him." After being seduced into sin in the Garden of Eden, the Lord asked Eve, "What have you done?"

> "'The Philistines will now come down on me at Gilgal, and I have not made supplication to the Lord.' Therefore I felt compelled, and offered a burnt offering.' Samuel said to Saul. 'You have done foolishly'" (1 Samuel 13:12-13).

To act foolishly is to live a life that leaves God out of it: "The fool says in his heart, 'There is no God'" (Psalm 14:1). Saul explained in this paraphrase: "When I saw the people were scattering from me and you weren't here by the time you were appointed to be and the Philistines were gathering together, planning to do something, I *had* to act. They said they were going to attack me at Gilgal."

WAITING ON THE LORD

Looking back over your own life, how often right after you came up with your own plan B, C, and D did God show up with plan A, but you had already messed it up? You were being tested, not because God needed information, but because He already knew but you didn't. He wanted you to see that all you do is talk a good game but when the pressure is on, you choose not to obey Him.

It's easy to trust God whenever we get paid favorably every two weeks but then, are we really trusting God through our employers? When the employer goes out of business, however, God is still in business. When the employer is bouncing checks, God is still rich beyond our wildest imagination. Since He promised to care for us before we got into that situation, He wants us to trust Him.

"But Lord, the bill has to be paid in two more days and I've just got enough for three lottery tickets." "Lord, if I can just steal this one time, I'll pay it back." And the Lord says, "Aren't you going to trust Me?" The point is that Saul had a promise that Samuel would be there in seven days. Samuel had an impressive track record of keeping his word. This was to show Saul he really wasn't made of what God wanted for a king.

> [13] And Samuel said to Saul, "You have done foolishly. You have not kept the commandment of the Lord your God, which He commanded you. For now the Lord would have established your kingdom over Israel forever. [14] But now your kingdom shall not continue. The Lord has sought for Himself a man after His own heart, and the Lord has commanded him to be commander over His people, because you have not kept what the Lord commanded you." [15] Then Samuel arose

and went up from Gilgal to Gibeah of Benjamin. And Saul numbered the people present with him, about six hundred men (1 Samuel 13:13-15).

If we don't pay attention and read with understanding, it could seem that God was being arbitrary here. After all, Saul only made one mistake and everyone makes mistakes. Why would God react so swiftly to reject Saul as king? When we look at Ephesians 1:11, we learn that God does everything after the counsel of His own will. According to His own will, God in essence said here, "I'm going to place a man after My own heart on the throne. This is My heart and decision to put this king in place." Did you catch that? God said the man He was going to put in place was the one He wanted in place after the counsel of His own heart and will. It was going to be God's decision and not the people's choice. David of course responded and pursued God wholeheartedly, but first and foremost, it was on God's heart to choose David.

It was on God's heart to choose you and because you are in His life and on His heart, He wants to be on yours. He wants you to respond in worship. You should be privileged to be in church when you think that you could instead be in hell. God chose to reach out to you, to rescue you and allow you to serve Him and read this Word to know you can live life on a different level. If you choose to disobey, there are consequences. It's not that God doesn't love you, but He loves you enough to allow you to feel the consequences for your disobedience.

It's not that complicated. Obey the Word of God. Trust His promises to you. Then you can live the rest of your life without regrets. I hear many people say they have no regrets. I have not done everything perfectly my whole life. We all have made choices and decisions we regret but you can determine that "From this moment on, I'm going to walk in His will. I want to live the rest of my life with no regrets. I wish I hadn't made some of those sinful choices I made, but I thank God that, despite of all those, He has rescued me and I can live the rest of my life making Him Lord of the days I have left. Amen!"

Lord, we are inspired by the life of Your faithful servant Samuel, and pray we might be used by You to have a similar influence in our generation. Help us not to sin against You by failing to pray for those persons we serve, whether or not we are pleased or disappointed by their behavior towards us or You. Help us to speak boldly and courageously every time You give us opportunity to challenge, convict, and lead those who are willing to follow us as we follow hard after You. In Jesus' name we pray, Amen.

FIRST SAMUEL 14-15

FOOLISH VOWS
AND REBELLIOUS PRIDE

The Bible tells us not to make vows foolishly, haphazardly, or thoughtlessly. It's better that we not make a vow than we make it and not keep it. What kind of vows have you made in your life? Vows are words of commitment that should never be shared or said without thoughtful consideration and resolute determination to honor the spoken words. There's a danger in making vows that don't honor the Lord. We must be humble enough to swallow our pride and renounce every self-defeating vow we have ever uttered. If we do so, we can become spiritually and emotionally healthy, able to serve the Lord rather than serve our own agendas.

I am intrigued by my study of Saul's life and not for the biblical information. I've learned from this study that it is entirely possible to be given everything we need to succeed and still fail, largely because of something I call the sinkhole syndrome. We see pictures of sinkholes with houses and automobiles in them. At one time, those were on solid ground, but then one day the earth underneath was gone and everything collapsed into the holes that created. The collapse is sudden, but what was going on underneath didn't happen overnight. It had been going on for a while.

We must guard against our own sinkholes, things in our own lives that erode and decay after we did a good job of hiding them. Then all of a sudden, there's a collapse. God had been warning us that we should be addressing that weakness by the power of the Holy Spirit. Sometimes the enemy doesn't bother us in our areas of weakness because we're already weak. He goes after our strengths. When we are strong in an area, we make the mistake of thinking we really don't need to pray about something. We can get up and talk without praying because we can communicate. We have skills, charisma, gifts, and talents. We can get by relying on our areas of strength without being dependent on the Lord. That's another sinkhole, an accident waiting to happen.

Saul had been given everything he needed to succeed but he failed miserably because he stopped trusting the Lord, instead trusting his own kingdom agenda fueled by his own gifts, talents, and resources. This caused him to make foolish vows. He was a prideful, arrogant man, but he didn't start off that way. God will put us in situations where we can see what He already knows is going on in our hearts. If we worked as hard on being real on the inside as we do trying to fool people on the outside, we could become strong in Christ.

The struggle between Israel and the Philistines was an ongoing battle that took place over decades. When we get to chapter 14, Saul was trying to figure out what he was going to do. How was he going to attack? Was he going to attack? We saw in the last chapter that he didn't wait on Samuel, his army was disappearing, and he felt he needed to do something.

JONATHAN ACTS IN FAITH

Saul had a son named Jonathan, a good leader who trusted the Lord. He wasn't worried about the size of the enemy's army because he knew God was able to deliver Israel:

> ¹ Now it happened one day that Jonathan the son of Saul said to the young man who bore his armor, Come, let us go over to the Philistines' garrison that is on the other side. But he did not tell his father. ² And Saul was sitting in the outskirts of Gibeah under a pomegranate tree which is in Migron. The people who were with him were about six hundred men (1 Samuel 14:1-2).

The Lord is never hindered by the number of people available for Him to use. God thinned out Gideon's army so they wouldn't think they were victorious because of how many soldiers they had. Samson singlehandedly brought down the house as his last act and took with him many Philistines. God doesn't need a multitude, just one person who will surrender and let Him do miraculous things through that person. Jonathan was ready to go get the Philistines. He was ready to climb up and fight. Jonathan saw everybody else standing around and he said, "Let's go do this." Notice he did not tell his father.

In order to accomplish God's will, there will be times when you have to respectfully work around leaders like Saul. If on your job or in some other setting the leadership is not on point and you know something has got to be done, you have to work around your leadership. You want to be respectful and biblically submissive, but you know you have to work around the current leadership because you want God's work to get done. You know it won't happen with them in charge.

That's what Jonathan did. He didn't tell his father what he was going to do, only his armor bearer. They started to climb up the mountains that were named Bozez and Seneh, which meant *shining* and *pointed*. We read in 1 Samuel 14,

> [6] Then Jonathan said to the young man who bore his armor, "Come, let us go over to the garrison of these uncircumcised; it may be that the Lord will work for us. For nothing restrains the Lord from saving by many or by few. [7] So his armorbearer said to him, "Do all that is in your heart. Go then; here I am with you, according to your heart. [8] Then Jonathan said, "Very well, let us cross over to these men, and we will show ourselves to them. [9] If they say thus to us, 'Wait until we come to you,' then we will stand still in our place and not go up to them. [10] But if they say thus, 'Come up to us,' then we will go up. For the Lord has delivered them into our hand, and this will be a sign to us. [11] So both of them showed themselves to the garrison of the Philistines. And the Philistines said, "Look, the Hebrews are coming out of the holes where they have hidden." [12] Then the men of the garrison called to Jonathan and his armor bearer, and said, "Come up to us, and we will show you something."
>
> Jonathan said to his armor bearer, "Come up after me, for the Lord has delivered them into the hand of Israel." [13] And Jonathan climbed up on his hands and knees with his armor bearer after him; and they fell before Jonathan. And as he came after him, his armor bearer

killed them. [14] That first slaughter which Jonathan and his armor bearer made was about twenty men within about half an acre of land (1 Samuel 14:6-14).

The Philistines saw these two men coming up and thought they were coming to surrender. The next thing they knew, those two had climbed right into their camp and took down 20 soldiers before anyone knew what was happening. Those who trust have learned that the size of the army doesn't matter to God. He supplies the power and gives the victory. We never limit God to what we think He might do in any given situation. Let Him surprise you with how He works things out.

There was chaos in the Philistine camp. People were hearing reports they had been invaded and didn't know it was only two men. They started running around looking for someone to fight, and they actually attacked each other after God sent an earthquake. Some of the Hebrews who had sold out before then joined in the battle. And the next thing anyone knew, there was a huge victory because two men had the courage to say and think, "God doesn't need a lot of us. He just needs us to trust Him. He's already told us He'll give us the victory over our enemies if we trust Him."

Saul got with the program, so to speak, after he saw what was going on in the Philistine camp. You have been in similar situations where you came up with a great idea and then your boss or others wanted to take credit for it. Saul and his army fought and won. Then Saul called for the priest to get some help and after a while he changed his mind and moved ahead into the battle. First Samuel 14:23 tells us that the Lord saved Israel that day, and the battle shifted to Beth Aven.

That would not have happened if Jonathan had not taken the initiative. If you find yourself in that difficult situation, you say, "Lord, I want to respect the leader but something has to be done and he or she is not being sensitive to what You want to accomplish." I guarantee God will show you how to get it done.

A FOOLISH EDICT

In verse 24 states, "And the men of Israel were distressed that day, for Saul had placed the people under oath, saying, 'Cursed is the man who eats any food until evening, before I have taken

vengeance on my enemies, so none of the people tasted food.'"
There is a danger in making rash nonbiblical vows. Saul put a
curse on anybody who ate until after the battle was won. He
weakened his own soldiers who desperately needed sustenance.
There was no logical reason for him to make such a statement. It
was a foolish vow.

As you read the rest of the story, you learn at one point his
men became so hungry that they violated all the kosher commands
of God about handling blood properly (God says the life of all flesh
is in its blood.) God demanded blood always be treated respectfully
because it signifies life. The men were so hungry that they started
eating raw meat. They were that hungry, famished, and weak.

Meanwhile, Jonathan had not heard about the edict, so
he had eaten some honey and was refreshed, strengthened, and
revived. Saul found out about it, and in his pride and arrogance
he was ready to kill whoever violated his command not to eat,
including his own son.

The point here is that foolish vows need to be renounced.
They are self-serving and destructive, and they sometimes jeop-
ardize relationships. Your behavior today may be affected by an
inner vow you made that needs to be renounced. Saul went
through a process to find out who violated his commands. We
read in 1 Samuel 14,

> [37] So Saul asked counsel of God, "Shall I go down
> after the Philistines? Will you deliver them into the
> hand of Israel?" But He did not answer him that day.
> [38] And Saul said, "Come over here, all you chiefs of
> the people, and know and see what this sin was today.
> [39] For as the Lord lives, who saves Israel, though it be
> in Jonathan my son, he shall surely die." But not a man
> among all the people answered him. [40] Then he said to
> all Israel, "You be on one side, and my son Jonathan
> and I will be on the other side." And the people said to
> Saul, "Do what seems good to you." [41] Therefore Saul
> said to the Lord God of Israel, "Give a perfect lot." So
> Saul and Jonathan were taken, but the people escaped.
> [42] And Saul said, "Cast lots between my son Jonathan
> and me." So Jonathan was taken (1 Samuel 14:37–42).

In case you're not familiar with this practice called casting lots, there is a proverb that says, "The lot is cast into the lap, but its every decision is from the Lord" (Proverbs 16:33). Basically, it was like the roll of the dice. God would use what came up to show who was guilty or innocent. Also, the priest he had certain gems on his garment that would reflect light to show His will. What Saul was saying, "Lord, show me who it is who has violated my vow. I don't care if it's my own son. Whoever did it is going to die." Jonathan was identified as the one who had eaten. This was Saul's own son who helped him get victory over his enemies.

> 43 Saul said to Jonathan, "Tell me what you have done. And Jonathan told him, and said, "I only tasted a little honey with the end of the rod that was in my hand. So now I must die! 44 Saul answered, "God do so and more also; for you shall surely die, Jonathan." 45 But the people said to Saul, "Shall Jonathan die, who has accomplished this great deliverance in Israel? Certainly not! As the Lord lives, not one hair of his head shall fall to the ground, for he has worked with God this day. So the people rescued Jonathan, and he did not die (1 Samuel 14:43-45).

Some of you have said I will never let another woman or man tell me what to do. "I will never submit. I will never marry another one who looks like this or who talks like that." If God didn't direct you to say that, you had better stop telling God what you're going to do or not do, or who you're going to be with or not be with. Those are not biblical vows. Those are your own way out of a situation you found yourself in. God is trying to send you people who can help you, but because you made a promise 20 years ago that you would never do this or that, you're ruining your life and future by limiting your relationships. You're still not doing it for the glory of God or for His purposes. It's not for His kingdom, it's for your kingdom. You want to maintain control of your own life, but how is that working for you up to this point?

Some of you witnessed terrible role models in your home. You said you would never put yourself into a similar situation, never trust anybody to take care of you. Did God tell you to make that vow? At the end of the day, you need to trust God with the people in your life. Trust God to heal your hurts and stop being so toxic in your relationships. If you're not careful, you will do like Saul and destroy people who God is sending to help you. Jonathan was there to help his dad and his dad was ready to kill him. As we move on, we will see that David was doing everything he could possibly do to help Saul. What did Saul want to do but to kill David? Why?

He was jealous. We can be jealous of people who are more gifted than we are. A former pastor asked me once, "Why should I or anyone be jealous of a person who is gifted and could help me and glorify God." God decides who gets the gifts for His kingdom, for His glory, and for our good. So why are we jealous when somebody can do something better than we can? Learn from them. They are helping us grow.

PARTIAL OBEDIENCE IS DISOBEDIENCE

As we proceed through this chapter, we see that the war continued. Let's jump over to chapter 15 now where we will see that partial obedience is still classified as disobedience. It's better to do what the Lord commands than to do what makes you look good. Samuel also said the same to Saul:

> [1] Samuel also said to Saul, "The Lord sent me to anoint you king over His people, over Israel. Now therefore, heed the voice of the words of the Lord. [2] Thus says the Lord of hosts: 'I will punish Amalek for what he did to Israel, how he ambushed him on the way when he came up from Egypt. [3] Now go and attack Amalek, and utterly destroy all that they have, and do not spare them. But kill both man and woman, infant and nursing child, ox and sheep, camel and donkey (1 Samuel 15:1–3).

Saul was going to spare the kingdom of Amalek because he wanted to show off his conquests and humiliate them, even though God had given orders for their execution. Specific orders from the Lord must always be obeyed or we suffer consequences. Look again at how the specific order was. There was no room for misunderstanding or confusion, for God said to destroy them *all*.

Why did God direct Saul to destroy the Amalekites? They

had always been antagonists of Israel and God had given him more than enough time to repent. Centuries earlier, the Israelites were coming out of Egypt on the way to Canaan and went through the land of the Amalekites. The Amalekites attacked the women, children, the weak, and infirm, and they did it with a rear attack. It was brutal, heartless, and cruel (see Exodus 17:8-13). God gave them time to repent but their attitude never changed. They kept attacking and fighting God's people and God's agenda. God determined their time was up.

You may understand that the adults should be eliminated but why the children? As cruel as it sounds, God was actually rescuing them by not allowing them to grow up to become like their parents who were God's enemies and thus be lost forever. Have you ever thought about that? He actually delivered them from being raised up to become God haters like their parents by taking them before they got to that age.

God told Saul to destroy them all. We have no such command today as Christians. We have never been commanded to physically destroy our neighbors as some tried to do in the name of Christ through the Crusades and other so-called holy wars—and there was nothing holy about them. We are to love and pray for them. We are to try and win them to Christ, but we are never commanded to wage this kind of holy war, like the Jews were told to do.

> [4] So Saul gathered the people together and numbered them in Telaim, two hundred thousand foot soldiers and ten thousand men of Judah. That sounds a whole lot better than the 600 he had in the previous chapter. [5] And Saul came to a city of Amalek, and lay in wait in the valley. [6] Then Saul said to the Kenites, "Go, depart, get down from among the Amalekites, lest I destroy you with them for you showed kindness to all the children of Israel when they came up out of Egypt. So the Kenites departed from among the Amalekites (1 Samuel 15:4-6).

Before the order to execute them, Saul told the Kenites to vacate the premises for he didn't want to destroy them because they had treated Israel fairly. All the Amalekites had to do to get the same treatment was to repent and do what God wanted them to do. They too could have been spared. When God brings a hammer down, He's already given people plenty of time to repent. We see the end result, but we don't know how many times God had told them to stop. Then the God of patience says that's about enough, timeout, game over and we think, *How could God have done such a thing?* The fact that we are still here proves He shows grace and mercy to sinners.

> [7] And Saul attacked the Amalekites, from Havilah all the way to Shur, which is east of Egypt. [8] He also took Agag king of the Amalekites alive, and utterly destroyed all the people with the edge of the sword. [9] But Saul and the people spared Agag and the best of the sheep, the oxen, the fatlings, the lambs, and all that was good, and were unwilling to utterly destroy them. But everything despised and worthless, that they utterly destroyed (1 Samuel 15:7-9).

Didn't God say not to leave anything? Saul decided to spare the king and keep some of these animals, especially the good ones. The problem was God had not instructed Saul to do that. Disobedience grieves the heart of the Lord and the hearts of those who care about God's will being done.

> [10] Now the word of the Lord came to Samuel, saying, [11] "I greatly regret that I have set up Saul as king, for he has turned back from following Me, and has not performed My commandments. And it grieved Samuel, and he cried out to the Lord all night (1 Samuel 15:10-11).

Samuel knew this was coming but it was still painful. Notice God said it broke His heart to see what Saul was doing. God has feelings as we do. He experiences love, joy, and heartbreak when we don't do what we are supposed to do. Do you know why? It's because He loves us so much that He doesn't like to see us hurt ourselves. Every time we sin, every time we think we know more than He does, we're not just hurting ourselves, we are breaking His heart.

> [12] So when Samuel rose early in the morning to meet Saul, it was told Samuel, saying, "Saul went to Carmel,

and indeed, he set up a monument for himself; and he has gone on around, passed by, and gone down to Gilgal. [13] Then Samuel went to Saul, and Saul said to him, "Blessed are you of the Lord! I have performed the commandment of the Lord. [14] But Samuel said, "What then is this bleating of the sheep in my ears, and the lowing of the oxen which I hear?" (1 Samuel 15:12-14).

This was the second time Saul saw Samuel coming and greeted him all happy and smiling: "I did exactly what God wanted me to do. Aren't you proud of me?" Samuel said, "If you had done what God told you to do, I wouldn't hear these animals." And Saul said, "They have brought them from the Amalekites, for the people spared the best of the sheep and the oxen, to sacrifice to the Lord your God; and the rest we have utterly destroyed."

[16] Then Samuel said to Saul, "Be quiet! And I will tell you what the Lord said to me last night." And he said to him, "Speak on. [17] So Samuel said, "When you were little in your own eyes, were you not head of the tribes of Israel? And did not the Lord anoint you king over Israel? [18] Now the Lord sent you on a mission, and said, 'Go, and utterly destroy the sinners, the Amalekites, and fight against them until they are consumed.' [19] Why then did you not obey the voice of the Lord? Why did you swoop down on the spoil, and do evil in the sight of the Lord?" (1 Samuel 15:16-19).

In essence, Samuel said, "Saul, way back when you weren't all that, didn't God give you glory and honor and opportunities? When you were little in your own eyes, look what God did. Now you think it's all about you and your kingdom and you decide whether or not you're going to do what God wants you to do."

A Personal Application

It's interesting to discuss Saul, but you should go home and look in the mirror. Think back to when you didn't have all that you have and how God established and set you up. Think of your diligence when you first got saved, when you were on fire for the Lord. You got what you wanted and now you pick and choose how you're going to obey God.

^{20} And Saul said to Samuel, "But I have obeyed the voice of the Lord, and gone on the mission on which the Lord sent me, and brought back Agag king of Amalek; I have utterly destroyed the Amalekites. ^{21} But the people took of the plunder, sheep and oxen, the best of the things which should have been utterly destroyed, to sacrifice to the Lord your God in Gilgal (1 Samuel 15:20-21).

Saul denied any wrongdoing on his part, instead claiming he did what God wanted him to do. It was the people who made him do what he did. Whose decision was it to spare the king? It was Saul's. Who had the authority to make the soldiers destroy everything the way God told him to do? It was Saul. Poor leaders like Saul shift the blame to others instead of taking responsibility for their own sinful choices. At some point, we need to stop blaming others for what we do.

People-pressure influences and intimidate us. Others may sweet-talk us or feel bad for us, but at the end of the day God holds us accountable for what we do or don't do so. We have to stand in front of the mirror and say, "I exercised my will to disobey and I am responsible." It doesn't matter who didn't love, support, or encourage you, you decided to do whatever you did, and God says that's on you. Jesus never let people talk Him into doing anything out of God's will. He demonstrated how to do that through His yielded humanity and by the power of the Holy Spirit. That means we can do the same. That's not easy. We may lose some friends or a job along the way, but we don't have to sin against God. If we do, it's on us.

Saul claimed that he brought the animals back so he could sacrifice them to the Lord. That sounded impressive and spiritual, but the Lord had said He didn't want or need those sacrifices. We are all pretty good at giving God things He doesn't want. Have you ever noticed the stuff some people donate to church and charities? God gets the old car, while you get the new car. They think, "This isn't good enough for my house, so I'll give it to the church. Here God, here is my $20 purchase but where's my $200 write off?" If it's not good enough for your house, then why is it good enough for God's house?

²² So Samuel said: "Has the Lord as great delight in burnt offerings and sacrifices, As in obeying the voice of the Lord? Behold, to obey is better than sacrifice, And to heed than the fat of rams. ²³ For rebellion is as the sin of witchcraft, And stubbornness is as iniquity and idolatry. Because you have rejected the word of the Lord, He also has rejected you from being king" (1 Samuel 15:22-23).

Never minimize the sins of rebellion and stubbornness. Those actions expose a heart that it is rejecting Christ, and the outcome will be tragic if repentance does not occur.

What Saul did was the same as witchcraft. He partially obeyed and God indicated that was idolatrous and self-serving. Don't laugh at your stubbornness or rebellion. Don't dismiss your partial obedience, but consider how God views it. God says it's ugly. Who are we to decide how fully we will obey His commandments or which ones we will obey? We all do it. We don't want to give, serve, or be faithful. We don't want to be committed and go all in. We hear a voice saying to us, "Aren't you satisfied with a little bit of God? You give more than your neighbor. You give more than you used to give." Is that what He asked for when He was on the cross? How much did He offer then? He offered it all and we cannot do any less.

¹⁰ Now it happened, as Jesus sat at the table in the house, that behold, many tax collectors and sinners came and sat down with Him and His disciples. ¹¹ And when the Pharisees saw it, they said to His disciples, "Why does your Teacher eat with tax collectors and sinners?" ¹² When Jesus heard that, He said to them, "Those who are well have no need of a physician, but those who are sick. ¹³ But go and learn what this means: 'I desire mercy and not sacrifice.' For I did not come to call the righteous, but sinners, to repentance." (Matthew 9:10-13)

⁷ But if you had known what this means, 'I desire mercy and not sacrifice,' you would not have condemned the guiltless. ⁸ For the Son of Man is Lord even of the Sabbath" (Matthew 12:7-8).

We instinctively give up stuff we can do without anyway. That's why it doesn't read sacrificial offering on our church's giving envelope. Instead, we put tithes and offerings. In most cases, we are not giving sacrificially. It's just the tip of the iceberg of what we have and what we know we can do without. We can give this to the Lord and still buy all the electronic toys, clothes, and other stuff we want. It's not a sacrificial gift at all. It's an ease-our-conscience donation.

There was a bit of conviction on the part of Saul as he had a stand-in-front-of-the-mirror moment:

> [24] Then Saul said to Samuel, I have sinned. For I have transgressed the commandment of the Lord and your words, because I feared the people and obeyed their voice. [25] Now therefore, please pardon my sin, and return with me, that I may worship the Lord." [26] But Samuel said to Saul, "I will not return with you, for you have rejected the word of the Lord, and the Lord has rejected you from being king over Israel.

> [27] And as Samuel turned around to go away, Saul seized the edge of his robe, and it tore. [28] So Samuel said to him, "The Lord has torn the kingdom of Israel from you today, and has given it to a neighbor of yours, who is better than you. [29] And also the Strength of Israel will not lie nor relent. For He is not a man, that He should relent. [30] Then he said, "I have sinned; yet honor me now, please, before the elders of my people and before Israel, and return with me, that I may worship the Lord your God." [31] So Samuel turned back after Saul, and Saul worshiped the Lord (1 Samuel 15:24–31).

That chapter ends with King Agag thinking he was home free, only to have Samuel execute him.

PRIDE

Pride causes us to want to look good in the eyes of people rather than pleasing the heart of God. If we reject the Lord, we are going to experience the Lord rejecting us. Saul was concerned whether Samuel would go out with him in front of the people and perform the act of worship so that everything looked like it was well. Saul didn't want to confess his sin and be disgraced in front of people. He begged Samuel to accompany him to make him look royal so the people would think Samuel approved of his decisions. Samuel went with him but informed Saul that God had already torn the kingdom from him, just like Saul had torn Samuel's robe.

Saul continued to sit on the throne for almost fifteen more years, even though God had rejected him. He was just keeping the chair warm until David grew up. He had the title, but he was marking time until God put His man on the throne. There are some in leadership positions who really aren't leading because God has indicated He's through with them since they didn't want to let Him work through them. They get to cash their paychecks but there is nothing happening. That must be horrible to realize they are placeholders when they could have been the man or woman of God if they had only decided to wholeheartedly obey Him.

They turned their back on God long enough until He said, "I'm finished." They are alive and their heart is still beating, but there's nothing going on with them or through their ministry or leadership. When that happens, they become jealous of other people who are serving God and are taking advantage of the opportunities they forfeited. Like Saul, they care about looking good on the outside when God is more interested in heart matters. We break God's heart when we care more about our kingdom than about the kingdom of God.

I cannot study King Saul without realizing any one of us, myself included, could make that choice at any time because we don't want to do what God says, and then we squander opportunities. We have been given everything we need to succeed. We are children of God and have the same Holy Spirit living in us that raised Jesus from the dead. How much more do we need to do God's will? We need to get ourselves out of the way and do His will. We need to vacate our thrones and let God have His way to let His kingdom come and His will be done. This throne of life is not a game as some portray, but is serious business, for our futures are determined by who sits on the throne of our lives—the Lord or our own stubborn, unbroken will.

As we close this chapter, join with me in praying this prayer:

God, You are aware of our sinkholes, shortcomings, weaknesses, and vulnerable areas of temptation. We pray in the name of Jesus Christ that You would help us keep our eyes on You and help us surrender ourselves afresh to You. Help us learn to obey You wholeheartedly and to wholly surrender to You so we can be more concerned about Your kingdom coming and Your will being done.

Father, we pray for those who are in spiritual prison because they made vows they can't seem to renounce and break free from. They are hindered from living the fullness of joy in Christ because of unhealthy and unholy vows they made to themselves out loud or in their minds and hearts. We pray You would bring to our remembrance promises we made that were not according to Your will. Break their power, Lord, and cancel their curse. Lord, we pray we would be able to honor the righteous vows we made to you and to one another so Your will may be done in us and through us. Amen.

LEARNING TO SEE FROM GOD'S PERSPECTIVE

¹ Now the Lord said to Samuel, "How long will you mourn for Saul, seeing I have rejected him from reigning over Israel? Fill your horn with oil, and go; I am sending you to Jesse the Bethlehemite. For I have provided Myself a king among his sons." ² And Samuel said, "How can I go? If Saul hears it, he will kill me." But the Lord said, "Take a heifer with you, and say, 'I have come to sacrifice to the Lord.' ³ Then invite Jesse to the sacrifice, and I will show you what you shall do; you shall anoint for Me the one I name to you." ⁴ So Samuel did what the Lord said, and went to Bethlehem. And the elders of the town trembled at his coming, and said, "Do you come peaceably?" ⁵ And he said, "Peaceably; I have come to sacrifice to the Lord. Sanctify yourselves, and come with me to the sacrifice." Then he consecrated Jesse and his sons, and invited them to the sacrifice (1 Samuel 16:1-5).

There are life events that cause people to accuse God of doing something wrong. It fascinates me when sinful humans criticize the sinless, perfect, and holy God as though He has made a mistake or treated them badly. That goes to show that we don't always see things from His perspective.

As we look into chapter 16, we see that God is about to choose the man who will replace Saul. The Lord's process for choosing can be confusing unless we know what He's looking for. Samuel was obviously grieved over what Saul's leadership—or lack of leadership—had done to the people. God told Samuel to stop mourning for Saul. He wanted him to go and anoint the person God had chosen as Saul's successor. Notice the Lord said, "I have provided for myself a king among Jesse's sons."

Then notice how Samuel reacted. This was Samuel, the renowned judge of Israel, the one who was respected by everyone in Israel saying, "I can't do that. Saul will kill me if he finds out I've anointed someone else to be king." Does that strike you as odd? Do you see how being in charge had gone to Saul's head? We later see that David had to fear for his life too, and here we see that same fear in Samuel's life as well. That is the power a poor leader can have over the hearts and minds of good people.

We saw earlier that He had already decided to pick a man after His own heart and the counsel of His will. We also learned that David was a man who pursued God wholeheartedly. Did he mess up along the way? Yes, but the direction of his life was on the right course so every time he fell, God picked him up. It's one thing to fall whenever we are going in the right direction, quite another to fall whenever we are going the wrong way. God will get us up if we are going the right way.

Now here's where it appears that God suggests Samuel do something deceptive to avoid Saul's wrath. God directed Samuel to say that he was present in the area to offer a sacrifice while he was really going to anoint a new king. The only person who needed to know about this was David.

Godly leaders learn how to share truth selectively and withhold information that will do more harm than good. God is showing us how not to reveal truth to those who are enemies of the cross and would then use that information to harm others. Jesus never lied. He either told the truth or He didn't answer. That's not being deceptive, just wise. Would you tell Islamic radicals where the Christians were hiding so they could be killed?

I've had this conversation with Christians who say we are supposed to always tell the truth. They say if asked that question, we should say, "Yes, they're right over there." We don't have to tell things that would deliberately get others harmed and do a disservice to the will of God. For this reason, God told Samuel not to tell Saul he was going to anoint David as king.

Some of us say too much of the wrong thing. Things we shouldn't say we speak and things we should share we don't talk about. We need to learn to say what needs to be said and withhold information that would be harmful to the cause of Christ or others. We can do that without lying.

ANOINTING

Let me make a few comments about the concept of anointing. The word *anointing* basically means to be empowered by the Holy Spirit for your ministry or vocational ministry. Jesus was filled with the Holy Spirit and anointed for His public ministry at His baptism. It's the word we use to say that the Holy Spirit is empowering someone to do something specific for Him.

How can you tell if someone is anointed? There will always be some results if someone has been anointed to do something. People either respond in a positive or negative way, but the anointed person won't go unnoticed. Jesus never went unnoticed. People loved or hated Him, but they could not ignore him. The same was true for Paul's ministry. Wherever Paul went, there was going to be either revival or riots. There was always a response because he was anointed to do what God called him to do.

Saul did not have the anointing of God on his life. God gave him every opportunity. God changed his heart so he had the potential to be a good leader but he kept rejecting God's will and purpose. Therefore, David was to become the anointed one.

Notice verses four and five that when Samuel showed up, the people were nervous. They asked him if he was coming in peace. Keep in mind, Samuel was the judge of Israel, and he was making an unexpected visit. They thought maybe they had messed up and God was sending His prophet to bring judgment on their house. Samuel calmed their fears and said he was there to offer sacrifice. Then in verse six, Samuel found himself at Jesse's home:

> ⁶ So it was, when they came, that he looked at Eliab and said, "Surely the Lord's anointed is before Him!"
> ⁷ But the Lord said to Samuel, "Do not look at his appearance or at his physical stature, because I have refused him. For the Lord does not see as man sees; for man looks at the outward appearance, but the Lord looks at the heart" (1 Samuel 16:6-7).

Most of us have heard this verse all our lives, yet still work harder on our outward appearance than we do on our hearts. We could be an hour late for church, not because we're studying and praying but because we're getting dressed and trying to look good. *Which of my 15 suits should I wear? I have to match my tie and shoes!* Suddenly it takes three hours to get ready to go to church. There is no time to pray or read the Scriptures. This verse indicates it's not that important to look good on the outside.

FAITHFUL IN A LITTLE

When Samuel arrived at Jesse's home, Jesse's first son looked good, so right away Samuel's assumed he was the one. The nation was going through a dilemma because they had chosen a leader who looked good, and it was time for them to understand God's criteria for leadership. Then we read in verse eight that a son named Abinadab came in, but he wasn't the one. Shammah came by, but it wasn't him. By verse ten, seven sons had come in and none of them were the anointed one. The Lord kept telling Samuel, "That's still not the one."

In verse 11 Samuel asked if all the sons were present? Jesse indicated there was one more, the youngest who was out keeping the sheep. This was the one God wanted but the mindset of the whole family was that it couldn't be him, not the youngest one and the mama's boy. They didn't even regard him as a possibility, but that's the exact one God wanted.

Why wasn't David in the room? He wasn't invited because he was too young. He was in the field being faithful on his job. How we handle menial tasks is a good indicator of how we will handle bigger assignments as Jesus taught:

> [10] "He who is faithful in what is least is faithful also in much; and he who is unjust in what is least is unjust also in much. [11] Therefore if you have not been faithful in the unrighteous mammon, who will commit to your trust the true riches? [12] And if you have not been faithful in what is another man's, who will give you what is your own?" (Luke 16:10-12).

Stop seeking to be famous and start looking to be faithful. Jesus said the one who is faithful in the little things will be faithful in the bigger things. Why do we miss that? If you steal $10 when nobody's looking, do you think God is going to allow somebody to ask you to watch $1,000,000? You have already shown you cannot be trusted.

God is looking for people who are faithful in the little

things and details. When the camera are not on, how do you serve? When nobody's watching you, how do you serve? When you are not in the spotlight, how do you serve? You said you were going to do this, that, and the other. Did you? If you're not faithful in the little things, don't expect God to give you the big assignments. David was out there being faithful to his task because that was his lifestyle.

As a matter of fact, you'll see in the next chapter that he was so faithful to his job that he actually killed a lion and a bear in hand-to-hand combat to protect the sheep. Did you ever see a lion? Did you ever fight a bear? Would you take on a lion or bear to protect some sheep? That's what God was looking for.

This young man's mindset was that he was there to shepherd and protect the sheep and he was willing to fight off wild animals to do it. How many people do you know who would do that? That is the kind of heart God is looking for. If David took his job that seriously when it came to shepherding sheep, he would do it when he was a shepherd over peoples' lives.

You should be the best person at your job as far as how you do it. Doesn't the Bible tell us that we just do our jobs for the glory of God? You are His representative; you should not be the one showing up an hour late for work three times a week or calling in sick when you are the healthiest person in the company. That must stop.

AFTER THE ANOINTING

Jesse admitted there was one more son who was out with the sheep. God said that's the one, go get him. The whole process was held up until David could get there. David didn't know what was going on or why he was being summoned. His father and brothers didn't know either. They did not think he was worthy to be there, but God indicated David was the one. They introduced him to Samuel and he was ruddy, bright-eyed, and good-looking:

> [12] And the Lord said, "Arise, anoint him; for this *is* the one!" [13] Then Samuel took the horn of oil and anointed him in the midst of his brothers; and the Spirit of the Lord came upon David from that day forward. So Samuel arose and went to Ramah (1 Samuel 16:12b-13).

The narrative ends there without telling us how David's family reacted, what Samuel did next, or what changes took place in David, if any. The next verse does not report that David went and took over the throne. David was anointed and he went right back to taking care of the sheep. God was with him as he went, however, because this young man had a heart for the Lord.

A person's heart and mind are impossible to assess with human resources or by human standards, but the Lord is able to see and reveal what is otherwise hidden. Is God pleased with what he sees going on in your heart and in my heart? We often talk about how embarrassing it would be if we put everybody's thoughts on the screen during the service. We sit and nod our approval at the preacher and say amen, but what are we really thinking about in our heart? Would we want that up on the screen? I don't know how many people would show up if they knew all their thoughts were to be displayed in high definition on the screen.

Jeremiah 17:9 says the heart is deceitful above all things and incurably wicked. Only the Spirit of God can help us know what's really going on inside of us. He's looking to see if we really care about worshiping and serving Him, or about looking good when the camera is on us.

Anointed means you are empowered to do His job. God's power is available for all who will serve, but power alone does not guarantee results. God gave Saul everything he needed but he still failed miserably. It's not enough to have the power available from God. If your heart isn't right and pursuing Him, you will fail even though He has given you everything you need to succeed. That's why you must stay in step with the Holy Spirit and walk every step of this journey in obedience to the Lord.

Any one of us could wake up any day and make a wrong decision that will shipwreck everything we have been working. Do you think about that when you're driving? You may have been driving safely for the last five or fifty years. You better do it every time you're behind the wheel or everything you have done before can be lost in a moment. Stay faithful, moment-by-moment, step-by-step, for God's power is there but you must still make sure your heart stays in tune with His.

David was anointed but he went right back to caring for

the sheep. It was going to be fifteen years before he became the king. Could you do that? Could you be patient after God revealed that you were going to be the king? David was about to go through the hardest times a young man could possibly endure after he discovered he was anointed to be king. Saul used him and then tried to kill him. Saul hunted him down like a wild animal. He would be living in caves and running for his life. He would question God about why he was going through all kinds of trials.

THE PRICE OF LEADERSHIP,
THE COST OF OBEDIENCE

Leadership is more than looking good when the camera is on and people are watching. If you're really doing something for the Lord, I guarantee the enemy has a target on your back. You better stay in step with the Holy Spirit. David was anointed and most people still didn't know that God's hand was upon him.

There is another instance where the ignorant or uninformed could accuse God of wrongdoing. In 1 Samuel 16, we read,

> [14] But the Spirit of the Lord departed from Saul, and a distressing spirit from the Lord troubled him. [15] And Saul's servants said to him, "Surely, a distressing spirit from God is troubling you" (1 Samuel 16:14-15).

People may wonder and ask, "How can an evil spirit come from a holy God?" The answer is that the Lord is sovereign over all spirits. He created Satan who turned into Lucifer when he chose to sin, but he is still under God's control. You may not like what he gets away with, but if God wasn't sovereign over Satan and his demons, we wouldn't be having a church to go to. They would have killed us while we were on the way to worship. God is sovereign but in His sovereignty, He still allows demons to do what they think they are doing to destroy God's purposes. God uses those attacks to bring people to themselves. Consider this account from the book of Job:

> [6] Now there was a day when the sons of God came to present themselves before the Lord, and Satan also came among them. [7] And the Lord said to Satan, "From where do you come?"

So Satan answered the Lord and said, "From going to and fro on the earth, and from walking back and forth on it."

⁸ Then the Lord said to Satan, "Have you considered My servant Job, that there is none like him on the earth, a blameless and upright man, one who fears God and shuns evil?"

⁹ So Satan answered the Lord and said, "Does Job fear God for nothing? ¹⁰ Have You not made a hedge around him, around his household, and around all that he has on every side? You have blessed the work of his hands, and his possessions have increased in the land. ¹¹ But now, stretch out Your hand and touch all that he has, and he will surely curse You to Your face!"

¹² And the Lord said to Satan, "Behold, all that he has is in your power; only do not lay a hand on his person." So Satan went out from the presence of the Lord (Job 1:6–12).

We see in that passage the enemy had to go before God to get permission to attack Job. Nothing has changed. When the Bible says an evil spirit from the Lord came on Saul, it means God allowed it to happen, and here's why it happened in Saul's case. Saul's constant rejection of the Lord's will for his life led him to be tormented by demons. Everyone noticed that Saul was losing his mind, and demonic spirits were affecting him:

¹⁶ Let our master now command your servants, who are before you, to seek out a man who is a skillful player on the harp. And it shall be that he will play it with his hand when the distressing spirit from God is upon you, and you shall be well." ¹⁷ So Saul said to his servants, Provide me now a man who can play well, and bring him to me." ¹⁸ Then one of the servants answered and said, "Look, I have seen a son of Jesse the Bethlehemite, who is skillful in playing, a mighty man of valor, a man of war, prudent in speech, and a handsome person; and the Lord is with him." ¹⁹ Therefore Saul sent messengers to Jesse, and said,

"Send me your son David, who is with the sheep"
(1 Samuel 16:16-19).

After his encounter with Samuel, David had gone back to
care for the sheep. We then learn he had great musical skills and
was also a brave man and mighty warrior. He had already distinguished himself even though he was still quite young and spoke
and conducted his business well. What was he doing? Running
a corporation? No, he was still taking care of the sheep. Most of
us would not settle for that if we had the resume David had. We
would demand to be up front, large and in charge. David was
still doing what he was put in charge of doing, something he was
assigned to do. He was gifted, faithful, and talented, but he was
waiting for his time.

The word got out that David was different. When we
look for leaders, we automatically look for a mature adult who
is ready to step in the next day. God always starts with a child.
Nobody other than Adam and Eve has ever been born as an
adult. God always starts with the child and begins to develop
them at an early age. That's why it is important that we as adults
model correct behavior in front of our children. We don't know
who God is getting ready for His purposes, and our job is not to
hinder them but to help them get ready for what God is prepar-
ing them to do.

[19] Therefore Saul sent messengers to Jesse, and
said, "Send me your son David, who is with the
sheep." [20] And Jesse took a donkey loaded with bread,
a skin of wine, and a young goat, and sent them by his
son David to Saul. [21] So David came to Saul and stood
before him. And he loved him greatly, and he became
his armorbearer. [22] Then Saul sent to Jesse, saying,
"Please let David stand before me, for he has found
favor in my sight." [23] And so it was, whenever the
spirit from God was upon Saul, that David would take
a harp and play it with his hand. Then Saul would
become refreshed and well, and the distressing spirit
would depart from him (1 Samuel 16:19-23).

David came in and played music to soothe Saul's spirit. It
seems that certain kinds of music hinder demonic oppression and

help us draw near to God. Certain kinds of music calm our spirits, and certain kinds of music invite demons to come in and agitate or oppress our minds and spirits. There are certain things we listen to that take us places we should not be going any longer. There is some music that will help us get closer and nearer to the Lord, like praise and worship songs.

God invented love so love and romantic songs can be good too, but the message is important in that music. *Me and Mrs. Jones* wasn't on God's all-time hits list. *All I Want is a One Night Affair* wasn't written by the Holy Spirit. We must be careful concerning the messages we are receiving and what kind of music is delivering them to us.

Even when we are not trying to memorize words, we do it subconsciously when we listen to music. We were playing some music the other day from back in the day when my wife and I were younger. We hadn't heard some of the songs in 20 or 30 years, but as soon as the music kicked in, we knew the words even though we did not intentionally memorize those words.

Are you teaching your children Scripture? Teach them music to go with it and they will subconsciously start to remember the words, which will help their spirits. Satan doesn't like being around when people are praising God. That's why we are told to do it all the time because if we lived with an attitude of praise and worship, we wouldn't be so vulnerable to demonic attacks. We would keep our flesh under better control.

David was used to soothe Saul's spirit and yet there were times when the music had to stop. When it did, Saul grabbed a javelin and tried to run it through David. Saul was wide open to demonic invasion because every time the Spirit of God wanted to come in, Saul didn't have room for Him. This happened because he was more concerned about the kingdom of Saul than the kingdom of God.

That is an ongoing problem with some of us. We are energetic to pursue things we want instead of what God wants. Why do we do those things? Do you feel a sense of conviction when you look at your checkbook and see where you spend most of your money? We pay four times the money for an electronic toy than a book. Why is that? We shell out $700 for a television, but then won't take a class for which the book is $14. The book is going to help us grow in grace and in the knowledge of Jesus Christ, while God only knows what the television will do.

God was saying in 1 Samuel 16, "I'm here. I'm looking at your heart. I'm looking at what they're putting on your heart. Your heart is telling Me along with your checkbook what really matters to you." He's looking for a reflection of Himself when He studies you. Does He see that?

Pray this prayer with me:

> *Lord, we are often convicted of the choices we make not to pursue You the way we should. We surrender ourselves afresh. Father, we thank You that You chose us and gave us the privilege of following and serving You. Long before we gave You a first thought, we were already on Your heart. We thank You for that.*
>
> *We pray You would help us fully surrender to You. I pray for those who don't yet understand what job assignment You have for them. I pray they would open their hearts and be ready to receive the anointing You have for them. I pray they would give themselves to it wholeheartedly. I pray we will want to serve You more energetically than we have to this point in our lives. We want to give You our best because You gave your best.*
> *Amen.*

FIRST SAMUEL 17

KILLING YOUR GIANTS BY TRUSTING IN JESUS

In this chapter, we are going to learn how to kill our giants by trusting in Jesus. It can be a challenge when we look at a passage of Scripture that some of us have known since childhood. We may read and think, *Oh yeah, I've heard this before.* The word of God, however, always promises there is more to see and learn than the last time we looked. In twenty years, as you mature in your faith, I guarantee you this same passage of Scripture will show you something you previously didn't notice. Let's look at 1 Samuel 17 like it's the first time we have ever read about David and Goliath, but more importantly, the first time we have studied the God of David.

Most of us have had the unfortunate experience of being bullied at some point in our lives. Maybe you used to be a bully. It's a bad feeling when you are intimidated and taken advantage of while powerless to do anything about it. You want to do something but just don't know what to do. We have discovered that the bullies who go around angry all the time are scared and empty inside so they try to control others with their abrasive attitude and violent outbursts. The Bible says that anger rests in the bosom of a fool (see Ecclesiastes 7:9). I hope you don't walk around angry all the time. If you do, you need to immerse yourself in the word of God so you can get the peace that passes all understanding only Jesus Christ can provide (see Philippians 4:7).

As we look at the passage, the children of Israel were being intimidated by the Philistine army, especially by one giant of a man named Goliath. There are 58 verses in chapter 17, but let's focus and highlight just a few of these verses. You may want to read the chapter through before reading on.

There had not been a whole lot of fighting going as we begin the chapter even though the armies of Israel and the Philistines were set for battle. There were just a lot of wolf tickets being sold, which is street slang for threats of action. Goliath was the main one who was doing the wolfing.

These two armies were gathered together for battle on the slopes of the mountain with a valley in between. Goliath was calling out for somebody, anybody, from Israel to come and take him on. It is interesting that when we began this look at First Samuel, Israel clearly stated they wanted a king to lead them into battle like all the other nations had. Here was a perfect scenario for that to play out, for the Philistines had sent out their biggest man to fight. Logic says Israel's biggest man should have gone out to meet Goliath since the Bible reported that Saul was head and shoulders taller than anybody in Israel. Who did those people elect as their king? It was Saul. Saul was there but we don't see him rushing into the battle to fight Goliath.

Goliath appeared to be more than nine feet tall. The Bible tells us how heavy his helmet, armor, shield, and battle equipment were. This was one big, strong man who was armed and ready for battle, calling out for someone to challenge him.

> [8] Then he stood and cried out to the armies of Israel, and said to them, "Why have you come out to line up for battle? Am I not a Philistine, and you the servants of Saul? Choose a man for yourselves, and let him come down to me. [9] If he is able to fight with me and kill me, then we will be your servants. But if I prevail against him and kill him, then you shall be our servants and serve us." [10] And the Philistine said, "I defy the armies of Israel this day; give me a man, that we may fight together." [11] When Saul and all Israel heard these words of the Philistine, they were dismayed and greatly afraid (1 Samuel 17:8-11).

At certain times in the history of warfare, armies sent out their best men rather than engage in endless bloodshed. Whoever won the duel would win on behalf of his entire army and the other side would admit defeat and surrender. That is a beautiful and accurate picture of what happened for us through Jesus Christ. He was our representative and took our sins upon Himself. He conquered death, hell, the grave, Satan, and everything else. He represented us and now invites us to participate in His victory like we had fought the battle ourselves. For those who choose Satan to be their representative, they participate in his defeat.

TAUNTING THE PEOPLE OF GOD

This battle took place in Israel's territory. Just as the Philistines constantly harassed Israel and invaded their space, we frequently let the enemy camp out in our territory. Every once in a while, we should get flat-out embarrassed about how we let Satan set up camp in the territory of our hearts and minds where the Spirit of God wants to give us victory if we would yield to Him. It's as if somebody is stomping around in our backyard daring us to come out and do anything about it. That's what Goliath was doing to the nation of Israel, and that's what Satan is doing to some people. We need to let Jesus represent us and get the victory.

Verse 12 tells us that David was the son of that Ephrathite of Bethlehem Judah named Jesse. The Bible mentions a few cities named Bethlehem, just like there's a number of cities named Cleveland. Here the Bible was being specific. This was a small town less than ten miles from Jerusalem, the eventual birthplace of Jesus. David and his family grew up in Bethlehem, Jesse with his eight sons, and verse 13 tells us, "The three oldest sons of Jesse had gone to follow Saul to the battle. The names of his three sons who went to the battle were Eliab the firstborn, next to him Abinadab, and the third Shammah."

David was not there in the army because he was at home taking care of the sheep. It's interesting that Goliath referred to the Israel army as the servants of Saul. In reality, Israel's army should have been known as the servants of Jehovah. If they were only fighting for Saul, they had no power. If they were God's army, they could not lose.

David was given the task of taking some food and refreshments to the front lines where he could check on his brothers to see how the battle was going and report back to his father. For days, nothing really happened except they had to listen to Goliath and his relentless intimidating threats: "And the Philistine drew near and presented himself forty days, morning and evening" (1 Samuel 17:16).

Everybody was dressed for battle and in the right place

at the right time, but nobody was fighting. Day after day, Goliath issued the challenge and every day Israel went home terrified. Can you imagine the horrible feeling of being powerless day after day? Yet some of us know that feeling. For days, weeks, months, and years, we have sat virtually paralyzed, knowing something needs to happen and we didn't know how to make it happen. Satan is taunting us, and we don't know how to respond.

It would be like going to a heavyweight boxing match and one of the fighters standing in a ring, calling out to the audience, "Come on, let's fight. Winner take all!" You look at him, then look at yourself and think, *That's not going happen. I don't want that fight. I value my health and life too much.* These were not civilians or noncombatants, however; these were the armies of the living God who were promised victory so long as they did what God wanted them to do.

Goliath was there day after day, but nobody was taking him on. David arrived with a different attitude than anyone else had in Israel's army. He was not chosen to be part of that army, even though chapter sixteen identified him as a mighty man of war. This little shepherd boy was not afraid of a good fight, and hings began to happen as soon as David arrived on the scene.

> [25] So the men of Israel said, "Have you seen this man who has come up? Surely he has come up to defy Israel; and it shall be that the man who kills him the king will enrich with great riches, will give him his daughter, and give his father's house exemption from taxes in Israel. [26] Then David spoke to the men who stood by him, saying, "What shall be done for the man who kills this Philistine and takes away the reproach from Israel? For who is this uncircumcised Philistine, that he should defy the armies of the living God?" (1 Samuel 17:25-26).

The word was out that the king, who was in no hurry to take on Goliath, vowed that anybody who defeated Goliath could marry his daughter. What's more, he and his father's household would not have to pay taxes any longer. That's a bit of incentive there. Can you imagine the president being your father-in-law and never having to pay taxes, both you and your family? That's quite a reward. It looked good until they had to look at Goliath. *Maybe I'll choose another girl and pay my taxes! At least I'll be alive!*

DAVID WAS DIFFERENT

The only man out here who was not scared was David. He was choosing his battles carefully and Goliath was one of them but his brothers were not happy: "Now Eliab his oldest brother heard when he spoke to the men; and Eliab's anger was aroused against David, and he said, 'Why did you come down here? And with whom have you left those few sheep in the wilderness? I know your pride and the insolence of your heart, for you have come down to see the battle'" (1 Samuel 17:28).

David's brother was saying in essence, "What you doing out here little boy? Who is watching those few little sheep you're supposed to be watching? You are so proud, conceited, and arrogant. You came down here not to help us, not to check on us, only to mock us." Eliab was speaking out of his own insecurities. David's brothers were jealous and insecure, so they took it out on him. They were bullying their brother even though Goliath was bullying them.

We must ignore people's remarks about us when they misunderstand our intentions. It hurts when we come to do some good for somebody and they turn it around against us. David chose not to fight that battle with his brothers because that's not the reason he was there. He came out to see who it was who had the nerve to defy the armies of the living God. Satan was trying to get David's own brothers to distract him so he would start defending himself—to fight against them instead of the enemy.

It's hard to swallow your pride sometimes, especially when someone is saying things you know are wrong. Your response should be, "You know, I don't have time for that. I'm here to do God's business. I'm not worried about your opinion." If you worry about people's opinions, you will never get God's will done. Even believers will try to sidetrack you. If you are faithfully doing what God wants you to do, you will be amazed at the ways He provides so you can fulfill your assignment with real honor.

32 Then David said to Saul, "Let no man's heart fail because of him; your servant will go and fight with this Philistine." 33 And Saul said to David, "You are not

able to go against this Philistine to fight with him; for you are a youth, and he a man of war from his youth." [34] But David said to Saul, "Your servant used to keep his father's sheep, and when a lion or a bear came and took a lamb out of the flock, [35] I went out after it and struck it, and delivered the lamb from its mouth; and when it arose against me, I caught it by its beard, and struck and killed it. [36] Your servant has killed both lion and bear; and this uncircumcised Philistine will be like one of them, seeing he has defied the armies of the living God." [37] Moreover David said, "The Lord, who delivered me from the paw of the lion and from the paw of the bear, He will deliver me from the hand of this Philistine" (1 Samuel 17:32-37).

Notice what David said. There were times when these wild animals would come and take one of his sheep and he would go after it. Have you ever seen an animal, not just on the hunt, but one that has already taken its prey? They don't like to be bothered. We are not talking about a wild dog, but about lions and bears. David went after them and rescued his sheep. What would you have done? Perhaps you would have said, "I'm sorry I lost three sheep today!"

He took on a lion and a bear. The language of the text says that whenever a ravenous beast came after one of his sheep, David would fight with his hands and God would let him win. "If God let me defeat a lion and a bear to protect sheep, I don't know if this Philistine has anything different coming. This is personal. He is defying the armies of the living God. He is insulting God himself. We can't let this happen!" That's confidence in the Lord, and Saul said, "Go for it!" Saul was glad to have David do the work Saul should have been doing.

[38] So Saul clothed David with his armor, and he put a bronze helmet on his head; he also clothed him with a coat of mail. [39] David fastened his sword to his armor and tried to walk, for he had not tested them. And David said to Saul, "I cannot walk with these, for I have not tested them" (1 Samuel 17:38-39).

Saul was a big man, but David was a youngster. Saul's

armor did not fit David. He was not going to go out and fight Goliath while uncomfortable in somebody else's armor. David said, "You know what. Whenever I fought that lion and bear, I did not have this armor on. I cannot fight with it." God was going to equip him with what he needed for the fight. The other Israelites thought Goliath was too big to hit; David knew he was too big to miss.

> ⁴⁰ Then he took his staff in his hand; and he chose for himself five smooth stones from the brook, and put them in a shepherd's bag, in a pouch which he had, and his sling was in his hand. And he drew near to the Philistine. ⁴¹ So the Philistine came, and began drawing near to David, and the man who bore the shield went before him. ⁴² And when the Philistine looked about and saw David, he disdained him; for he was only a youth, ruddy and good-looking. He mocked him (1 Samuel 17:40-42).

Goliath had an armor bearer and look at what David had—or didn't have. Goliath was fully armed and had a helmet with a shield and sword ready for battle. David came at him with a slingshot, some rocks, and a big stick. Goliath said in 1 Samuel 16:43, "'Am I a dog, that you come to me with sticks?' And the Philistine cursed David by his gods. 'Are you going to come at me and fight me with a stick and some rocks?'"

Why did David pick out five stones? In 2 Samuel 21:18-22, we find a hint that Goliath had four brothers. We preachers like to creatively imagine aspects of some stories to bring out certain principles and in this case, we think that perhaps David knew the four brothers could also come at him, so the other four rocks were to take care of the brothers as well. That sounds good but we can't prove it.

The main point is that David was not afraid of this fight. He was confident not in himself, but in the God He served. It's one thing to be fighting for something near and dear to your heart that has nothing to do with the will of God. If you know it is something God wants to take place, you should take on that battle with confidence.

THE BATTLE IS THE LORD'S

The Lord has provided everything we need to fight victoriously. Make sure you use your God-given equipment for the battle. Saul's armor was useless to David. It wasn't what David needed for this battle. The Lord will show you what to use and what you need to win if you trust Him. The enemy may look intimidating, but he has weaknesses God will reveal to you when you engage him in spiritual warfare. Your five smooth stones will be provided by the word of God and the power of the Holy Spirit. That's all you need. God has provided you the weapons of warfare. We can read about that in a familiar passage about warfare in Ephesians 6:10-20, in which God describes how He has equipped us for battle. We need to use everything He has provided.

David was going against Goliath with a staff, a slingshot, and some rocks. I did a little research and have found out that skillful shepherds could sling stones at well over a speed of 100 miles per hour and were accurate up to fifty or sixty yards. It was like getting hit by a bullet. David was ready for the fight.

> [45] Then David said to the Philistine, "You come to me with a sword, with a spear, and with a javelin. But I come to you in the name of the Lord of hosts, the God of the armies of Israel, whom you have defied. [46] This day the Lord will deliver you into my hand, and I will strike you and take your head from you. And this day I will give the carcasses of the camp of the Philistines to the birds of the air and the wild beasts of the earth, that all the earth may know that there is a God in Israel. [47] Then all this assembly shall know that the Lord does not save with sword and spear; for the battle is the Lord's, and He will give you into our hands." [48] So it was, when the Philistine arose and came and drew near to meet David, please notice this that David hurried and ran toward the army to meet the Philistine (1 Samuel 17:45-48).

He didn't respond meekly by saying, "Okay, come on over, please?" No, he ran toward Goliath, a big man with a sword, shield, and an armor bearer.

When I watch boxing matches, at times the bell rings and one fighter runs to the center of the ring. Lots of times it is a ploy to distract his opponent. David had total confidence and ran towards Goliath, but it was no bluff. He was ready.

Our battle is the Lord's. We should run toward our spiritual assignments instead of running away from them in fear. Sometimes God gives us an assignment and we are totally intimidated. We find every excuse under the sun not to take on the challenges. Somebody has to take on the big challenges in life. Somebody has to take on the big challenges in ministry. Why not you?

The same Holy Spirit who empowers everybody else is available to you. Too often we're not like David. We are like the rest of Israel's army sitting back, thoroughly intimidated instead of thinking, *Wait a minute. This is something that God wants to happen. That means that I have to be successful.* Our job is to step up and be used of the Lord.

> [49] Then David put his hand in his bag and took out a stone; and he slung it and struck the Philistine in his forehead, so that the stone sank into his forehead, and he fell on his face to the earth. [50] So David prevailed over the Philistine with a sling and a stone, and struck the Philistine and killed him. But there was no sword in the hand of David. [51] Therefore David ran and stood over the Philistine, took his sword and drew it out of its sheath and killed him, and cut off his head with it. And when the Philistines saw that their champion was dead, they ran (1 Samuel 17:49-51).

David hit the giant where he was most vulnerable. He had a helmet on but there was an open spot on his forehead. By the grace of God and the direction of the Holy Spirit, the stone hit him right where he was defenseless. God will always show you where you can get victory. You must be man or woman enough to get up and fight the battle in the name of the Lord. The stone hit Goliath and down went Goliath. David ran over, took his own sword, and cut off his head just like he said he would.

I would have been satisfied to see Goliath go down. The thought of taking a sword, cutting off his head after killing him, and then carrying the head around would have been too much for me. Goliath was down and the armies of the Philistines were running.

> ⁵² Now the men of Israel and Judah arose and shouted, and pursued the Philistines as far as the entrance of the valley and to the gates of Ekron. And the wounded of the Philistines fell along the road to Shaaraim, even as far as Gath and Ekron. ⁵³ Then the children of Israel returned from chasing the Philistines, and they plundered their tents. ⁵⁴ And David took the head of the Philistine and brought it to Jerusalem, but he put his armor in his tent (1 Samuel 17:52-54).

After that, the army of Israel got involved in the battle. They chased the Philistines and gained a huge victory because of what one man had the courage to do. In many cases, it only requires one person to step out and trust God for victory and make it possible for others to share the rewards provided by the Lord. Because David had the courage to trust the Lord and take on Goliath, the whole army got to celebrate the victory. It didn't have to be David. It could have been someone else with courage to step up and do what God called him to do. David showed up and set the example.

The Holy Spirit may be knocking on your heart's door saying, "You know what? If you stand up and let me work through you, everybody around you will be blessed." The Church of Jesus Christ may be lacking courage in a certain area and God may be saying you are the one to reverse the trend. If you trust Him and set the example, then others can participate in the victory. David was that man.

> ⁵⁵ When Saul saw David going out against the Philistine, he said to Abner, the commander of the army, "Abner, whose son is this youth?" And Abner said, "As your soul lives, O king, I do not know." ⁵⁶ So the king said, "Inquire whose son this young man is." ⁵⁷ Then, as David returned from the slaughter of the Philistine, Abner took him and brought him before Saul with the head of the Philistine in his hand (1 Samuel 17:55-57).

I'm sure he was showing off to the other Israelites what

God had done by walking around with this head in his hand. Saying something like, "This is the man you were afraid of. This is the man that we let defy the armies of God. See what can happen when you trust God? See what God can do to His enemies? Come on fellas. Let's trust him!" "And Saul said to him, 'Whose son are you, young man?' So David answered, 'I am the son of your servant Jesse the Bethlehemite'" (1 Samuel 17:58).

Most people scratch their heads when they read that last verse and ask, "Wait a minute. Saul already had employed David to play music for him and soothe his spirit. Why did Saul seem like he didn't know David?" Perhaps Saul's attendants had "hired" David to play for Saul and Saul had not paid close attention to who was playing. It would be like an entertainer on a cruise ship, playing the piano and singing. You may enjoy the music but wouldn't recognize the musician the next day if you ran into that entertainer on the ship.

David was known for his musical skill, but he was going to a whole new level of fame with new challenges. Before long, there was going to be nothing but jealousy and resentment from Saul because soon they were going to be singing the praises of David, instead of the praises of Saul. Singing the praises of David was really declaring that God let David win. Ultimately, they congratulated David but they were really saying, "Look what God can do when somebody surrenders to the Lord." David knew the battle was the Lord's and there was no reason Goliath or anyone else should be able to stand against the armies of the true and living God.

The Lord is bigger than any obstacle you are facing. He wants you to trust Him for victory in every battle. He wants you to fight them, remembering the battle is not yours. The battle is the Lord's.

*Lord, we come to You on behalf of Your children
who are not as courageous as David was, and are
facing giant obstacles in their lives. We come to You
recognizing that many children and adults are being
victimized by bullies of all kinds, and ask that You
would show Yourself strong on their behalf. We pray for
those who are fighting battles that have nothing to do*

with Your will, and pray You would show them from this familiar story that You will grant victory to Your children when they are fighting the battles You have led them into. Help us be inspired by David's courage and passion for Your glory, and to realize how much larger You are than any giant we may face. In the name of the David's son and Lord we pray, Amen.

FINDING FRIENDS WHO REMIND YOU OF JESUS

There are some ugly statistics involving those involved in pastoral ministry. A 2010 survey by the *New York Times* indicated that members of the clergy are suffering from obesity, depression, and hypertension at rates higher than most Americans.

- One-third of all pastors say that to be in ministry is a hazard to their families;

- 40% of pastors and spouses suffer from burnout and unrealistic expectations;

- 52% of pastors say their spouses believe that being in pastoral ministries is hazardous to their family well-being and health;

- 80% of pastors say they have insufficient time with their spouse;

- 80% believe their pastoral ministry negatively affects their families;

- 90% work more than 50 hours per week;

- 70% say they don't have any close friends.

I distinctly remember entering pastoral ministry and being advised by some older pastors never to let anybody in the congregation know who my close friends were. If I had any, the rest of the congregation would get upset, causing problems. If that advice is correct, then men like me who desperately need close friends are being taught not to have any because it creates a ripple effect in the congregation. That's probably why we have those kind of statistics about burnout, depression, and discouragement in ministry. We all need friends and a few close friends. We need people who care about us and about whom we care in return.

I read a book in which the author pointed out that in

his opinion the only reason most people are in a pastor's life is because that pastor serves them. If he or she was not their pastor, they probably would not be their friend. They are only in a pastor's life because they need something from that pastor. That's horrible, but that is the reality for a lot of people in ministry.

We weren't designed to live our lives in isolation. Jesus had friends. He spent special time with Lazarus who was known as His friend, as were his sisters, Mary and Martha. The disciples were known as His friends and yet many of the pastors who are following and serving Jesus are hurting, lonely, and desperate, but they can't let anybody know what's going on. They can't get close to anyone.

DAVID'S FRIEND

There is a man who was an important participant in everything that happened in David's life after he began serving Saul. This man can be easily overlooked, but if it were not for him, there would not be much to read about in the life of David. That man is Jonathan, a life-saving friend to David, and the son of King Saul.

David would not have made it without Jonathan in his life. Jonathan was the kind of friend that reminds us of Jesus Christ. Jonathan was older than David. He was a brave and valiant man who led Israel in some victorious battles. He was a man who would have been king had his father known how to act. He was a man who had every right to resent David from a human perspective, yet he chose to be exactly the opposite. He spent his life saying, "I know God's hand is on you, David, and I've got your back." This friendship is described in three chapters, First Samuel 18 through 20.

Jonathan did not make constant demands on David, nor did David upon Jonathan. We can drive away a lot of potential friends by making a lot of demands and always being in need. Your friends will be attentive to you whether you request it or not, because they truly care about you and you should also care about them. Let's pick the story up after David's victory over Goliath:

> [1] Now when he had finished speaking of Saul the soul of Jonathan was knit to David and Jonathan loved him

as his own soul. [2] Saul took him that day, and would not let him go home to his father's house anymore. [3] Then Jonathan and David made a covenant, because he loved him as his own soul. [4] And Jonathan took off the robe that was on him and gave it to David, with his armor, even to his sword and his bow and his belt (1 Samuel 18:1-4).

Those with an agenda endorsing homosexuality as a lifestyle try to use this chapter and these verses to prove their argument. They maintain David felt a love for Jonathan that was better than the love of the woman. It states the souls of Jonathan and David were knit together. There's nothing mentioned about sexual activity. Instead, this is a description of what God intended and that's male bonding. It's men's fellowship in which men can actually share heart issues and love one another the way God intended without any sexual activity being part of it. Jesus loved the men He served, and I hope you don't dare believe He had homosexual issues.

BEING LIKE JONATHAN

Christ-like friends connect with your soul and they give their best for and to you. You can only knit a soul together when you share heart issues and care about similar things. Jonathan knit his soul together with David and declared that he was there for David—and then backed it up with action.

Jesus said in John 15:12, "This is my commandment, that you love one another as I have loved you." Jesus demonstrated His love for people. He didn't just say it, He demonstrated it through word and deed. If friends say they love you but never go out of their way to support you or your family, that's not the real thing. Jesus continued, "Greater love has no one than this, than to lay down one's life for his friends. You're my friends if you do whatever I command you why what I call you servants when they don't know what the Masters doing that I've called you friends all things that I've heard from my father I have made known to you" (John 15:13-14).

God actually wants us to be His friends. Yes, we worship, praise, and serve Him. We do what He tells us but He wants us to be His friends in the midst of those other realities. Some people don't understand why Abraham was called a friend of God, but it was because they shared life concerns with one another. Jesus said if we are only servants, we wouldn't know what was going on in the Master's mind. Servants don't know why they do what they do; they simply carry out what they are told. Jesus wants us to know what's going on in His heart and then have a friendship emerge from that.

Look again at what it says in 1 Samuel 18:4: "And Jonathan took off the robe that was on him and gave it to David, with his armor, even to his sword and his bow and his belt." Jonathan was doing something symbolic that indicated to David, "Yes, I am the son of King Saul and in a perfect world, I would be the next king of Israel. I know, however, God has chosen you and all that I have I give to you in support of God's choice." Isn't it interesting that in the previous chapter Saul tried to give David his armor and that didn't work? Then Jonathan clothed David and it seemed to fit perfectly. That is how it is with friends.

Jonathan surrendered to David just like Jesus wants us to surrender to Him. *Lord, I give up my right to my little kingship in my little kingdom and all that I have is Yours in absolute surrender.* That's a beautiful picture of Christ-like friendship.

> [5] David went out wherever Saul sent him and behaved wisely. And Saul set him over the men of war, and he was accepted in the sight of all the people and also in the sight of Saul's servants. [6] Now it had happened as they were coming home, when David was returning from the slaughter of the Philistine, that the women had come out of all the cities of Israel, singing and dancing, to meet King Saul, with tambourines, with joy, and with musical instruments. [7] So the women sang as they danced, and said: "Saul has slain his thousands, and David his ten thousands." [8] Then Saul was very angry, and the saying displeased him; and he said, "They have ascribed to David ten thousands, and to me they have ascribed only thousands. Now what more can he have but the kingdom?" [9] So Saul eyed David from that day forward (1 Samuel 18:5-9).

This passage describes what old folks used to call the evil

eye. Saul became insanely jealous of David when he realized that David was going to get the kingdom. God had said that would happen and it was clear God had set things in motion to make it happen. Christ-like friends don't become envious of their friend's success. The Bible tells us that if we walk uprightly, we will receive all God has ordained for us. The Bible also tells us the Lord God is a sun and as shield for us and He will withhold no good thing from those who walk uprightly—*if* we do what God has told us to do (see Psalm 84:11).

You will receive everything God has ordained for you to have, so you don't have to live your life in envy and jealousy of others. Saul could have had everything. All he had to do was obey God but he didn't, and then was upset with a man who obeyed. The sad reality is that Saul was vulnerable to demonic attacks for the rest of his days. We must not give a place for the devil to invade our hearts by being envious and jealous of anyone.

SAUL ABUSES DAVID

"And it happened on the next day that the distressing spirit from God came upon Saul" (1 Samuel 18:10). Our sovereign God has control over every angel and demon He created. Satan and his servants cannot get to anyone unless God for His sovereign reasons allows them access. This spirit came upon Saul and he began to prophesy in his palace. David played music as he did at other times and it would typically soothe Saul's troubled spirit. In this case, however, there was a spear in Saul's hand: "And Saul cast the spear, for he said, 'I will pin David to the wall!' But David escaped his presence twice" (1 Samuel 18:11).

David had to escape Saul's violent retaliation twice! You may think your boss is tough, but can you imagine trying to do your job and dodging spears at the same time? That was one of the realities of David's situation. Saul was afraid of David because the Lord was with him while He had departed from Saul. "Therefore, Saul removed him from his presence, and made him his captain over a thousand; and he went out and came in before the people. And David behaved wisely in all his ways, and the Lord was with him" (1 Samuel 18:13-14).

As we read the text, we learn that Saul kept sending David out to war for a reason: to have him die in battle. David was walking in the will of God and God protected him while Saul got angrier and more envious and jealous. (There is a slight difference between those two words, *jealousy* and *envy*. I can be jealous of what someone has. I don't want it myself, but I don't want to see them have it. When I am envious, it means that I *want* what they have.) That's a horrible way to live. God can give you everything you need to have so you can live a satisfying life, but still you choose to be jealous and envious of others.

Saul began to connive and plot to do away with David. Saul had promised his daughter's hand in marriage to David in return for killing Goliath, but he gave his firstborn daughter to someone else. He then saw that his daughter, Michal, loved David. He then thought, "I'm going to let her marry David and then I'll have a connection and entry point to get to him." David was humbled to be the king's son-in-law, but all that time, Saul was setting him up, using his own daughter to find an opportunity to kill David while David's intent was to serve Saul. David never did anything against Saul but Saul was continually trying to kill him. First Samuel 18:29 says, "Saul was still more afraid of David. So Saul became David's enemy continually."

That represents a long fall from grace for Saul who could have been a great king. God would have empowered and worked through him. Saul couldn't get past serving his own kingdom. The kingdom of Saul meant much more to him than the kingdom of God. That's where the title for this book comes from. That's the problem we deal with. The throne of your life is no game. If you don't make a conscious choice and concerted effort to move from your kingdom to God's kingdom, you will sit on the throne of your life, and make bad decision after bad decision.

We know we have problems like Saul. We really want God to help us with our own little kingdom but surrendering our right to rule and committing to His greater plan are difficult. That's why we need Christ-like friends, like Jonathan was to David, and we should be that kind of friend to other people.

Walk wisely at all times because there's literally a step between life and death. Jonathan realized that and said in in 1 Samuel 20:3-4,

> [3] Then David took an oath again, and said, "Your father certainly knows that I have found favor in your

eyes, and he has said, 'Do not let Jonathan know this, lest he be grieved.' But truly, as the Lord lives and as your soul lives, there is but a step between me and death." [4] So Jonathan said to David, "Whatever you yourself desire, I will do it for you."

David was under constant attack. One wrong move could have been the end of his life. In reality, that's the way it is for every one of us. We never know when we are about to take our last step. We need to walk in God's will every moment of every day and determine never to take a step out of God's will, because we don't know where that step might lead. I think of that every time I get in a car, every time I get on a plane. I never know so I want to make sure that every moment of every day I am doing what God has directed me to do.

Be busy doing what you believe God wants you to do because at any moment you can take that step between time and time eternal. If you prepare for that, then life looks a little different. If you're not prepared, then I suggest you get prepared right now. This could be your day of destiny.

Jonathan and David bonded together and they both realized that Saul, given the opportunity, would kill either of them if they let down their guard. The Lord never runs out of ways to protect us, His servants who have work to do, and He will use Christ-like friends to help us do so. That should be a comfort to us. You have supernatural protection because you are not finished with God's assignment. It's not by coincidence that we walk the streets safely. We need to recognize God has unfinished business with our lives and in the midst of danger, He keeps us safe.

SAUL'S CHILDREN PROTECT DAVID

Saul hated David but his son and daughter loved him. They both risked their lives protecting David from their father. Only God can do something like that and give you friends in high places. We read in 1 Samuel 19 that Jonathan was trying to talk his father out of killing David, reasoning with him that David was there to help. Saul promised to leave him alone but shortly thereafter, the demons got excited again and Saul tried to kill him once more.

⁸ And there was war again; and David went out and fought with the Philistines, and struck them with a mighty blow, and they fled from him. ⁹ Now the distressing spirit from the Lord came upon Saul as he sat in his house with his spear in his hand. And David was playing music with his hand. ¹⁰ Then Saul sought to pin David to the wall with the spear, but he slipped away from Saul's presence; and he drove the spear into the wall. So David fled and escaped that night. ¹¹ Saul also sent messengers to David's house to watch him and to kill him in the morning. And Michal, David's wife, told him, saying, "If you do not save your life tonight, tomorrow you will be killed." ¹² So Michal let David down through a window. And he went and fled and escaped (1 Samuel 19:8-12).

If you read the rest of the chapter, you learn that Saul's daughter used a statue to make it look like David was asleep in the bed. They came to kill him, but he was long gone, and Saul was outraged: "Then Saul said to Michal, 'Why have you deceived me like this, and sent my enemy away, so that he has escaped?'" Michal answered Saul, 'He said to me, 'Let me go! Or I will kill you?'" (1 Samuel 19:17-18).

The Bible records what people actually said, and we learn that people, both then and now, lie at times. You've probably experienced that situation more than once. You don't have the courage or faith to say the truth, but you have good intentions. Michal was trying to protect David but at that moment she felt like if she didn't say something to satisfy her crazed father, he was going to kill her. She had to make it look like David threatened her.

After that, Saul sent battalions of men after David and when you read the rest of the chapter, you will see that the Spirit of God came over them, and instead of being able to attack, they all went into a spiritual ecstasy and started prophesying and praising the Lord. Evil Saul did the same thing. God never runs out of ways to protect us. He can make His enemies praise Him whenever they don't want to. He protects David because David has unfinished business as king of Israel.

In chapter 20, this beautiful story continues of men being friends the way God intended them to be with no agenda or activity outside of God's will. Jonathan constantly offered himself to protect David. He devised a scheme to play out during a feast that David had no intention of attending. They knew Saul would wonder why David was absent and so they came up with a plan to determine Saul's true intentions and a way to signal David if the plan was evil.

It's tough dealing with people we love who have issues in their hearts and lives. We never know when they are going to have one of their bad or off days of demonic oppression, rendering us helpless and wondering what to do. The beauty of this story is that Jonathan was a man of God as was David, and they realized they were part of an eternal family that took precedent over blood relationships. Christ-like friends recognize the significance of God's family.

Throughout chapter 20, we see Jonathan finding ways to intervene for David to keep his father's wrath away from the man he knows God appointed king of Israel. Jonathan tried to honor his father and do the will of God, but he ended up between a rock and a hard place. He risked his life to protect David because he knew his father was out of God's will.

David was in God's will and Jonathan was going to be a friend to David, and his father would disrespect and insult him for it. When we read the text, depending on the translation, it says Saul got upset with Jonathan and called him the son of a perverse woman. Saul as the father picked the mother. How could he insult her and his son without insulting himself? Saul had a habit of blaming everyone but himself for whatever was going on in his life.

> [31] "'For as long as the son of Jesse lives on the earth, you shall not be established, nor your kingdom. Now therefore, send and bring him to me, for he shall surely die.' [32] And Jonathan answered Saul his father, and said to him, "Why should he be killed? What has he done?" [33] Then Saul cast a spear at him to kill him, by which Jonathan knew that it was determined by his father to kill David. [34] So Jonathan arose from the table in fierce anger, and ate no food the second day of the month, for he was grieved for David, because his father had treated him shamefully (1 Samuel 20:31-34).

The chapter ends with another beautiful passage about this friendship that society often tries to twist and pervert for its own agenda.

> [41] As soon as the lad had gone, David arose from a place toward the south, fell on his face to the ground and bowed down three times. And they kissed one another *(author's note: this was the Middle East, where it is still customary for men to kiss one another on the cheek)*. They wept together, but David more so. [42] Then Jonathan said to David, "Go in peace, since we have both sworn in the name of the Lord, saying, 'May the Lord be between you and me, and between your descendants and my descendants, forever.'" So he arose and departed, and Jonathan went into the city (1 Samuel 20:41-42).

Ancient kings had a horrible custom when a kingdom passed from one family to another. The new or conquering king would kill all the sons of the previous king so none of them would have a claim or try to take back the kingdom. David and Jonathan promised that they would not do that, vowing never to kill one another's sons or grandsons. Jonathan is a Christ-like friend, the kind of friend we all need but should also seek to be to others.

BE A FRIEND TO OTHERS

We can be selfish at times, thinking about what we can get out of our relationships. As Christians, we are supposed to be the exact opposite. We should be in relationships to give even if we get nothing in return. Being like Christ means we are always doing our best for what we can for others. David's story would have ended prematurely and quickly if Jonathan had not assumed the role and posture that he did.

It's a great honor to be called a friend of God. Abraham had that title. It's mentioned in James 2:23 and is a quote right out of Genesis. God makes it clear that He wants us to be His friends. If we are, we can then be Christ-like friends to one another. There are people who are hurting because they don't have Christ-like friends in their lives.

Why don't you look beyond your owns needs and see if

you can find somebody to love and let them know they are appreciated. When you try to meet the needs of others, it is the best way to get your own needs met. We have it backwards when we demand that others meet our needs or else we curtail or end the relationship. That's the way of the world. God directs us to give ourselves to others, to lay what we have on the line for others like Jonathan did for David.

When you do, watch how God fills the gaps in your life. I hope you're not one of those people who feel you don't have a close friend. There were years when I had a lot of friends, but my hectic schedule did not let me be involved with them as closely as I would have liked. Even now, I don't I feel I have the time to give them what they need. There is always important work to do. That's why people crash and burn and the reality is, if I had taken the time to connect, the work I am so absorbed in would be there when I come back. We need to be Christ-like friends for each other.

> *Lord Jesus, You have declared that You want us to not only be Your servants, but also to be Your friends. What a privilege to share heart issues with You. We pray we will be the kind of friend to others that Jonathan was to David, wanting the best for someone else, caring, protective, and encouraging others to fulfill Your purpose in their lives. Remind us, Lord, that as we seek to befriend others, You will enrich our lives with the kind of friends we need to help us through the challenges we would rather not face alone. Father, we ask that You help us remember the symbolic act of Jonathan surrendering his belongings to David, as a picture of our willingness to surrender to You as the One who has the right to rule. For Your glory and our good we pray in the name of our King Jesus, Amen.*

FIRST SAMUEL 21-22

THE FUGITIVE

If you have never read Samuel before, there is no movie that has the kind of drama and the relational mess that played out between David and Saul. Somebody could make a movie out of First and Second Samuel and viewers who didn't know the Bible would think it was a great screenplay. What we want to discuss in this chapter is the danger of allowing fear to overcome faith.

If you are remotely close to my age, you probably remember a weekly television show called *The Fugitive*—not the movie, but the weekly television show (it was actually based on a true story of a man from the Cleveland area). The show featured a doctor who had been accused of killing his wife and he was on the run from the authorities every week. He was regularly close to being caught or killed, and his whole life was a life of lies and deception because he felt that was the only way to keep going and prove his innocence.

By the time we reach 1 Samuel 21, King David was officially a fugitive for the remainder of the book. He was on the run, trying to elude King Saul who was hot on his heels. This man who was supposed to be leading the kingdom of Israel was spending his time chasing down David, who he perceived to be a threat to his throne. God had already anointed David as king, and it was just a matter of getting David ready so he would have the maturity to lead. Saul thought that if he killed David, he could prolong his time on the throne. He should have repented and done God's will and only then could he have continued to be king.

TURNING FROM FAITH TO FEAR

This represented a turning point in David's life, for it is at this time that David had to choose between walking in faith and living in fear. I don't want to be too hard on David for we all have issues in our lives that cause us to fear, but he made a few judgments and decisions that were costly not only to him, but also to those around him. He also walked at times in a magnificent display of faith.

Every person encounters things and situations in life that evoke an initial response of fear. It's how we respond that makes the difference. If you see an out-of-control pit bull running at you and someone across the street tells you not to be afraid, it doesn't help. Unless somebody stops that dog, you have every reason to feel fear.

Whenever God or one of His angels appeared in the Bible, the natural response to their holiness was to be afraid. Even a believer's first response when a divine being confronted them was fear and terror and therefore the angelic messenger would always say, "Fear not," along with some qualifying words, "for I am with you. Fear not because I am here to bless you. Fear not because. . . " There had to be a reason given to calm the fear.

The great I Am wants to remind us that we don't have to live in fear because He is with us. If we don't practice His presence and know Him personally, fear can cause us to make unhealthy decisions that will keep us from enjoying life. Some of you are making life decisions based on fear rather than faith. *What if my job is eliminated? What if my spouse leaves me? What if this happens, what if that happens?* There are legitimate reasons to be fearful but if you are not careful to put all those concerns back in the hands of the Lord who loves and has made promises to you, you will make all your life decisions based on fear instead of from faith. David made a few decisions out of fear.

ACTING DECEPTIVELY

By this time in our story, Saul had played a game of darts with David as the target, trying to pin him to the wall with a spear—and he did this on at least three occasions. It's only by the grace of God those spears missed David and hit the wall. Saul had also tried to kill his own son on a few occasions. David felt the only option he had was to run, even though God had protected him from the spears. God had also protected him when he took on Goliath, but at that time in his life, fear had overcome his faith and so he chose to run.

[1] Now David came to Nob, to Ahimelech the priest. And Ahimelech was afraid when he met David, and

said to him, "Why are you alone, and no one is with you?" ² So David said to Ahimelech the priest, "The king has ordered me on some business, and said to me, 'Do not let anyone know anything about the business on which I send you, or what I have commanded you.' And I have directed my young men to such and such a place. ³ Now therefore, what have you on hand? Give me five loaves of bread in my hand, or whatever can be found."

⁴ And the priest answered David and said, "There is no common bread on hand; but there is holy bread, if the young men have at least kept themselves from women." ⁵ Then David answered the priest, and said to him, "Truly, women have been kept from us about three days since I came out. And the vessels of the young men are holy, and the bread is in effect common, even though it was consecrated in the vessel this day."

⁶ So the priest gave him holy bread; for there was no bread there but the showbread which had been taken from before the Lord, in order to put hot bread in its place on the day when it was taken away (1 Samuel 21:1-6).

David came to the place where the priests were surprised to see David by himself, so one of the priests asked what he was doing there. David did not admit he was running from Saul, nor did he warn the priest to be careful what he did to help David because Saul, the madman, was chasing him. If Saul found out the priest helped David, it could lead to trouble, but David did not do that. Instead, David told a tale that the king sent him on some business with a crew and asked what they had to eat there.

Fear can lead to a lifestyle of deception and we see that here in David's life. He was a fugitive and felt compelled to lie rather than trust God for wisdom and protection. Previously he had gone to Samuel when he had issues with Saul, or he had prayed and asked the Lord what he should do. This time fear drove him and he went to where the priests were, fearing exposure and deciding not to tell the real reason he was there.

Does that scenario describe your life? Do you tell people

why you came to them and what you really need from them, or do you feel you can only share a little bit? You don't really want to confess you are afraid and running. Isn't it embarrassing when we look back and realize how we seldom tell people what is really going on in our lives? We weren't trusting God because we were walking in fear and not in faith.

Even when we are faithless, God is faithful to provide in unique ways. David asked them what they had to eat. When you are fugitive, the restaurant offerings get pretty slim. The priest told David that all they had was the bread of the presence or the showbread, which was dedicated for use only by the priests. David knew they rotated that bread every few hours to keep it fresh, so the bread the priests gave David was the bread removed from the table of God's presence. It was still good bread, sanctified for the priests' consumption. Before the priests gave David the bread, they asked if David and his men had been living holy lives. Jesus actually referred to this story in Mark 2.

> [23] Now it happened that He went through the grain-fields on the Sabbath; and as they went His disciples began to pluck the heads of grain. [24] And the Pharisees said to Him, "Look, why do they do what is not lawful on the Sabbath?" [25] But He said to them, "Have you never read what David did when he was in need and hungry, he and those with him: [26] how he went into the house of God in the days of Abiathar the high priest, and ate the showbread, which is not lawful to eat except for the priests, and also gave some to those who were with him?" [27] And He said to them, "The Sabbath was made for man, and not man for the Sabbath. [28] Therefore the Son of Man is also Lord of the Sabbath" (Mark 2:23-28)

The reason I point this out is that rituals were never intended to be more important than legitimate human needs.

In Mark 2, the legalists wondered how Jesus' disciples dared to work picking grain on the Sabbath—grain that didn't belong to them no less. Jesus replied with what I refer to as holy sarcasm. The men questioning Jesus had committed the Old Testament to memory, but He asked them if they had ever read the story of David visiting the priests. Of course they had read it; they probably had it memorized. Just because they read it, however, didn't mean they understood it, which was the point Jesus was trying to make. David had a legitimate need, went to the high priest, ate the bread designated for the priests, and didn't violate one of God's commandments.

Another example of this principle was the edict in the Law that stipulated people were to leave the corners of their field unharvested so the poor could come in and harvest food for themselves from the edges of the field. None of that was out of order on the Sabbath.

The Sabbath day was never meant to be a burden to men. It was meant to be a time to rest when people could reflect on the God who makes life possible every day. Jesus refuted their claim of Sabbath-breaking and told them they needed to discover what the Scriptures really said and taught. They were accusing Jesus of violating the Sabbath, but He was the Lord of the Sabbath. Some people today know what the Bible says, but they don't know what it means.

Returning to the story of David and the priests, we see that fear-based actions lead us to places outside of God's will for our lives: "Now a certain man of the servants of Saul was there that day, detained before the Lord. And his name was Doeg, an Edomite, the chief of the herdsmen who belonged to Saul" (1 Samuel 21:7).

Edomites were enemies of the Israelites. One of Saul's top dogs just happened to be present when David came for counsel and provision in his time of need. Because David was making fear-based decisions, he never realized he was stepping out of God's will. We wind up in places God never intended for us when we walk in fear and not faith. Wherever we go down the road of fear, we should not be surprised when someone is there who is inclined to harm rather than help us.

You won't necessarily meet those people when you go off partying or eating. There are some churches you can go and where everybody is not going to bless you. Satan sends folks to church. The best place to cause confusion is where the Word, the truth of God, is being taught. Satan has preachers and a lot of them. Some of them are well-paid, faithful, and committed to manipulating and taking advantage of people while perverting the gospel. He doesn't need to send people where the truth isn't being taught. He only has to plant a few where he knows people who are hurting come for help so he can take them off course.

How many people do you meet who say they don't go to church anymore because they went and someone did them wrong? They are turned off to Christ and the gospel because somebody who didn't represent Christ met them at church. That's why I preach Jesus. I have great people in my church, but as Paul said, "We don't preach ourselves, we preach Jesus Christ the Lord; we are his servants for Jesus sake" (2 Corinthians 4:5).

Doeg was there and he ran back to Saul to spill the beans and then David realized that he was not well-equipped to be living a life on the run so, "David said to Ahimelech, 'Is there not here on hand a spear or a sword? For I have brought neither my sword nor my weapons with me, because the king's business required haste'" (1 Samuel 21:8). David was still twisting the truth by lying and insinuating, "I didn't have time to grab my armor or my weapon. Is there anything I can use?"

> The priest responded, "'The sword of Goliath the Philistine, whom you killed in the Valley of Elah, is here, wrapped in a cloth behind the ephod. If you will want it, take it. For there is no other except that one here.' David said, 'There is none like it; give it to me'" (1 Samuel 21:9).

The priests were involved full-time in doing ministry for Jehovah so they didn't typically have any extra weapons around for people who needed one. The fact that they offered him Goliath's sword should have jogged David's memory into asking why he was so fearful. *The same God who protected me against Goliath can still protect me* should have been uppermost in his mind.

We all have those moments when we let fear overcome us even though we have many promises from God of His protection. In the moment we doubt, we don't trust. We forget God had bailed us out many times, but we are not sure if He can do it again. David's fear was going to lead them into hostile territory. Are your steps being guided by fear or by faith?

HIDING AMONG THE ENEMY

"Then David arose and fled that day from before Saul, and went to Achish the king of Gath" (1 Samuel 21:10). Gath? Why does that area with an unusual name sound familiar? It is because David killed a big man named Goliath who was from Gath.

Of all the places he might think twice about going was to Gath, for he had killed their hometown hero. His plan was to run for shelter in Goliath's home town? The people recognized David when he arrived and asked in verse 11, "Isn't this David, the king of the land? Isn't this the guy whose going to rule and reign in a little while? We've heard he has authority and responsibility. He's the one who took down Goliath and he's here." It was as if David had worn a Cleveland Browns jersey into a game against their archrival, the Pittsburgh Steelers.

The locals continued, "Didn't they sing of him and the servants of Achish said to him, "Is this not David the king of the land? Did they not sing of him to one another in dances, saying: 'Saul has slain his thousands, And David his ten thousands'?" (1 Samuel 21:11). They recognized David right away.

David's fear-driven steps had led him into hostile territory. What about you? Do you keep winding up in places where God doesn't want you to go, and then thinking, "Look what I got myself into!"

"David took these words to heart, and was very much afraid of Achish the king of Gath" (1 Samuel 21:12). David was afraid, fearing for his life. They knew him, and He was exposed and in danger. "So he changed his behavior before them, pretended madness in their hands, scratched on the doors of the gate, and let his saliva fall down on his beard" (1 Samuel 21:13).

He didn't see any way out except acting like a total fool, seeming like he was bipolar, schizophrenic, and demonized all at the same time. The distinguished, anointed, and famous David started scratching on a doorpost. This was the courageous man of Israel who was now afraid of them. David felt he had to take matters into his own hands and do something to protect himself. The best plan he could come up with was to act crazy.

A beard was important to a man in the culture of David's day. No man in their right mind would let saliva dribble through their beard. That was distasteful and dishonoring for any man to do. I was 60 years old before I was able to grow some facial hair. When I was in the Army, we were camped out one morning when the drill sergeant looked at me and said, "Morrison found time to shave this morning. What about the rest you guys?" I got everybody in trouble, but I was 21 and had never shaved a day in my life. Now that I'm finally old enough to grow a beard, my wife doesn't like it so I shaved it off. David acted like a madman, hoping that everybody would leave him alone—and it worked:

> [14] "Then Achish said to his servants, "Look, you see the man is insane. Why have you brought him to me? [15] Have I need of madmen, that you have brought this fellow to play the madman in my presence? Shall this fellow come into my house?" (1 Samuel 21:14-15).

In essence, the king said, "We have enough fools in this town. Get him out of here!" His fear-based actions led David into danger. He was not trusting God so he had to come up with something to get out of there. We all have those moments where we don't trust the Lord and we try to think ourselves out of our situation and circumstances. We lose sight of the promise God has given us. God promised David he would be king of Israel. That meant all of Gath and Philistia. The world could not take him out because God promised he would be king.

When the disciples were scared on the sea of Galilee because a life-threatening storm came out of nowhere, they woke Jesus up and said, "Don't you care that we are about to drown?" Jesus had promised them if they got into the boat, they would go to the other side. He didn't promise that they would get in the boat and drown in the middle of the lake. We have to remember God's promise so we don't get scared to death before we arrive. Are you struggling because you have lost sight of the promise and you are in the midst of the storm? Jesus says, "I didn't bring you here to drown. I brought you here to deliver on the promise I made." David had lost sight of that, and we do too. The Lord is faithful even when we are fearful. He will provide us with the help we need.

PEOPLE COME TO DAVID

As we move into chapter 22, we read

> [1] David therefore departed from there and escaped to

the cave of Adullam. So when his brothers and all his father's house heard it, they went down there to him. ² And everyone who was in distress, everyone who was in debt, and everyone who was discontented gathered to him. So he became captain over them. And there were about four hundred men with him (1 Samuel 22:1-2).

This is a beautiful passage. Notice what God was doing in his life. A few chapters earlier, David's own brothers were mocking him, not supportive of his presence or role. Then people slowly started to recognize that God's man was a fugitive, God started sending him a secret service and army, men he would train to be soldiers. Look at their qualifications. They were in distress, in debt, and discontent. That's what you need to build an army, isn't it? A bunch of folks with problems, who were discontent with their circumstances and in horrible situations. Nevertheless, God was leading them to David.

The kind of men coming to David in the cave provides a beautiful picture of us when we come to Christ and become a part of His army. The cream of the crop was not running to him, only those who were hurting, in debt, and in distress. They became his mighty men and eventually made up quite a powerful fighting force. When they first came, however, they did not have it all together.

We sometimes expect people to walk into our churches and have it all together. When we come to Christ, did we come because we had it all together? No, we were like those men. We were hurting but we came to Him and He empowered us. It is this empowering that caused us to live like He wants us to live. David was going to shape, mold, and train those men to become a great army. God sent these men to David when he was not making the best choices, but God used that to remind him he was a man on a mission. Despite his choices, God was sending him people so he was not alone. He was going to have an army with him from then on.

³ Then David went from there to Mizpah of Moab; and he said to the king of Moab, "Please let my father and mother come here with you, till I know what God will do for me." ⁴ So he brought them before the

king of Moab, and they dwelt with him all the time that David was in the stronghold.

⁵ Now the prophet Gad said to David, "Do not stay in the stronghold; depart, and go to the land of Judah." So David departed and went into the forest of Hereth (1 Samuel 22:3-5).

David took his parents back to Moab because he had some history there. He was the son of Jesse and Ruth was in his family line. He didn't know where life was going to take him, so he took care of his parents. Then God sent a word to him through the prophet of Gad not to keep hiding here, but to go back to Judah. Are you open to hearing a word from the Lord when you're walking in fear and not by faith, going to places where you have no business going? As a child of God, you should always expect God to speak to you. He may say go back to the place where you're fearful to return. He may say go back and face the challenge you are afraid of. The Lord told David to return to Judah. God said he was going to be king, so he was safe from Saul.

No matter what situation you find yourself in, be open to hearing and responding to a word from the Lord. Sometimes we get discouraged and don't want to hear from the Lord. We can't control what He says and we may not like it. We can actually get used to the situation we are in. We also may get used to controlling our situations and other people through crisis after crisis, and we enjoy seeing people reacting to our needs. Some people actually live like that. They have convinced themselves people will only be there if they have problems. Instead of getting to the place where they can help others, they always insist that others help them. There is a verse that says if you want friends thens show yourself to be friendly (see Proverbs 18:24).

DAVID'S LIES, LOST LIVES

We don't want to move from that kingdom of *me* where we are the head. We have been re-elected as head of our lives every time we run. We don't allow anybody to run against us. The throne—who is running our lives—is not a game. We all desperately need to make the transition from my kingdom to Thy kingdom.

⁶ When Saul heard that David and the men who were with him had been discovered—now Saul was staying in Gibeah under a tamarisk tree in Ramah, with his spear in his hand, and all his servants standing about him—⁷ then Saul said to his servants who stood about him, "Hear now, you Benjamites! Will the son of Jesse give every one of you fields and vineyards, and make you all captains of thousands and captains of hundreds? ⁸ All of you have conspired against me, and there is no one who reveals to me that my son (Jonathan) has made a covenant with the son of Jesse (*author's note: Saul did not even want to say his name*) and there is not one of you who is sorry for me or reveals to me that my son has stirred up my servant against me, to lie in wait, as it is this day." ⁹ Then answered Doeg the Edomite, who was set over the servants of Saul, and said, "I saw the son of Jesse going to Nob, to Ahimelech the son of Ahitub. ¹⁰ And he inquired of the Lord for him, gave him provisions, and gave him the sword of Goliath the Philistine."

¹¹ So the king sent to call Ahimelech the priest, the son of Ahitub, and all his father's house, the priests who were in Nob. And they all came to the king. ¹² And Saul said, "Hear now, son of Ahitub!" He answered, "Here I am, my lord." ¹³ Then Saul said to him, "Why have you conspired against me, you and the son of Jesse, in that you have given him bread and a sword, and have inquired of God for him, that he should rise against me, to lie in wait, as it is this day?" ¹⁴ So Ahimelech answered the king and said, "And who among all your servants is as faithful as David, who is the king's son–in–law, who goes at your bidding, and is honorable in your house? ¹⁵ Did I then begin to inquire of God for him? Far be it from me! Let not the king impute anything to his servant, or to any in the house of my father. For your servant knew nothing of all this, little or much" (1 Samuel 22:6-15).

The priest admitted he had seen David, but he was

confused because David was Saul's most faithful servant—or so he thought. The priest knew David to be Saul's son-in-law, so why wouldn't he help him? The priest could not see the problem.

> ¹⁶ And the king said, "You shall surely die, Ahimelech, you and all your father's house!" ¹⁷ Then the king said to the guards who stood about him, "Turn and kill the priests of the Lord, because their hand also is with David, and because they knew when he fled and did not tell it to me." But the servants of the king would not lift their hands to strike the priests of the Lord (1 Samuel 22:16-17).

Saul's servants had come to the point where they felt he was crossing the line of appropriate behavior. His son-in-law had been faithful to Saul. They saw there was obviously an issue between the two of them, but Saul's servants did not want to get involved. Then when Saul wanted them to murder the priests of God, they had to defy a direct order from their commander-in-chief. Doeg the Edomite was there, however, and he didn't have a lot of use or love for most Israelites:

> ¹⁸ And the king said to Doeg, "You turn and kill the priests!" So Doeg the Edomite turned and struck the priests, and killed on that day eighty-five men who wore a linen ephod. They wore the robe of the priest. ¹⁹ Also Nob, the city of the priests, he struck with the edge of the sword, both men and you and women, children and nursing infants, oxen and donkeys and sheep—with the edge of the sword. He killed everything he could put his hands on (1 Samuel 22:18-19).

I have read some commentators who try and justify Saul's actions because the priests were supposed to be loyal to the king. In their mind, if someone aided and abetted the enemy, then that meant they were not faithful to the head man, so he had the right to execute them. With all due respect, I'm not buying that interpretation.

You may remember a man named Eli in the first few chapters of First Samuel who had failed the Lord by not chastening his sons when they made a mockery of the worship of God. Their judgment was their descendants would not be able to continue as priests. God's word never returns to Him without accomplishing why He sent it, so guess who those 85 priests were whom Saul had executed? They were Eli's descendants!

Only one of those priests escaped. It's another example of how someone's decisions affect others for good or bad. You can in effect create generational blessings for all who come after you or make decisions that will cause problems for generations to come. Eli, the high priest, did so much wrong in the sight of God that his descendants were affected. Only one of them got away.

> [20] Now one of the sons of Ahimelech the son of Ahitub you, named Abiathar, escaped and fled after David. [21] And Abiathar told David that Saul had killed the Lord's priests. [22] So David said to Abiathar, "I knew that day, when Doeg the Edomite was there, that he would surely tell Saul. I have caused the death of all the persons of your father's house. [23] Stay with me; do not fear. For he who seeks my life seeks your life, but with me you shall be safe" (1 Samuel 22:20-23)

Notice that David made a 180-degree turnaround. The same man who had been running for his life was once again walking in faith. He felt responsible for what had happened to the priests and realized if he had given them a warning, perhaps they would still be alive. David was coming to his senses and felt responsible for all the deaths that took place in the household of priests.

DAVID COMES TO HIS SENSES

When necessary, you must acknowledge your actions that have brought harm to others. The Lord is faithful to forgive your sins, but he will hold accountable those who refuse to repent. You may have caused some people horrible pain and you need to say, "I confess I was wrong. I repent." That's all you can do, but the grace of God is sufficient, and the blood of Christ never loses its power. There is nothing you have done or can do that He will not forgive if you come to Christ. The only unforgivable sin is *not* coming to Christ. He will hold accountable those who continue to violate His will and refuse to repent.

It is true He said Eli's sons would die, but He still held

Saul responsible because he should not have done what he did by killing them. Then David told the priest who survived, "Stay with me. Don't be afraid. The one who's after you is also after me. You'll be safe as long as you stay with me." David wasn't so sure of that truth at the beginning of the chapter but he repented and changed his thinking.

The words spoken by David to Abiathar reflect the same protection we receive by staying close to Christ, who is our Protector. The enemy is after anybody he can get his hands on. He's been at war with God since the Fall. Jesus is the only place we are safe when we stay close to Him. He's our only protection.

It's disturbing to watch the news and see what's happening, not just locally but around the world. Politicians can't get the world out of the mess it is in. That is not happening until Christ comes back. The only safe place to be is in a saving relationship with Jesus Christ. You have a promise that until His Word for you is finished and fulfilled, nobody can get you. Jesus says, "Stay with me. You'll be safe." The promises and presence of God are enough to move us from living in constant fear to living in concrete faith. Are you going to continue to take steps of fear or to walk in a faith relationship with Jesus Christ? The choice is yours.

Lord, we pray for those who are living life on the run, hiding from those persons they may have harmed or who seek to do them harm. We ask for Your supernatural protection for them. We also pray for those who are running as fugitives from Your justice, thinking they can hide themselves to keep from facing You. We ask that You bring them from fear to faith in You and cause them to realize that You are the only One who can grant them the freedom they desire. Remind us that our choices always affect those who are in relationship with us and help us to be men and women of the truth. Thank You for the reminder from David's words to his men, that as long as we are with You, we shall be safe. We are grateful we will forever be safe with You. In Your glorious name we pray, Amen.

SPECIFIC ANSWERS TO SPECIFIC PRAYERS

We have been studying the topic of moving from my kingdom to Thy kingdom, which means we step down from ruling our own lives and accept God's rule in every aspect of life. As we have studied Saul and David, we have been searching for lessons to apply from what they did correctly and not replicate what they did wrong. We want to learn how to get out of the way so God's kingdom can be manifest in our lives. By doing so, we will see God's will accomplished through our life purpose. Many of the kings missed doing that. In this study, we have learned that Saul missed doing that. God wants us to realize that we need to let go of our little kingdoms and be involved in the coming of His kingdom.

We established in the last chapter that David could officially be labeled a fugitive. He had been anointed to be king of Israel, but he would have to wait for fourteen years before he actually had the privilege of sitting on the throne. While he was waiting, he went through some of the toughest times of his life. He was running for his life, threatened time after time, alone, abandoned, and forsaken, yet we see how God showed up and showed off time and again as He delivered David from every situation in which he found himself.

We have now come to 1 Samuel 23. We saw in the last chapter that God had sent an army of 600 men to be with David, some of whom would distinguish themselves to be known as David's mighty men. I like to call them his Secret Service or bodyguards. They were well-trained soldiers who were empowered and used by God to gain David victory after victory. As chapter 23 opens, even though David was being chased and attacked, he still had a shepherd's heart. When he heard about some fellow citizens who were in danger in Judah, he asked the Lord if He wanted him to get involved.

SPECIFIC QUESTIONS, SPECIFIC ANSWERS

David asked a specific question, expecting a specific answer from the Lord, and we can do the same. The word of God says in 1 Samuel 23,

> [1] Then they told David, saying, "Look, the Philistines are fighting against Keilah, and they are robbing the threshing floors." [2] Therefore David inquired of the Lord, saying, "Shall I go and attack these Philistines?" And the Lord said to David, "Go and attack the Philistines, and save Keilah." [3] But David's men said to him, "Look, we are afraid here in Judah. How much more then if we go to Keilah against the armies of the Philistines?" [4] Then David inquired of the Lord once again. And the Lord answered him and said, "Arise, go down to Keilah. For I will deliver the Philistines into your hand." [5] And David and his men went to Keilah and fought with the Philistines, struck them with a mighty blow, and took away their livestock. So David saved the inhabitants of Keilah. [6] Now it happened, when Abiathar the son of Ahimelech fled to David at Keilah, that he went down with an ephod in his hand (1 Samuel 23:1-6).

David was in danger so he was hiding in different places. He heard about the citizens of Keilah being attacked by their common enemy, the Philistines. David didn't say, "That's King Saul's job to take care of those people." Instead, he asked, "Lord, should I get involved in it? Do you want me to take on this assignment?" Sometimes we hear about needs, and we choose *not* to pray because God may tell us that He wants us to help. David received clear direction during challenging and dangerous times. We will also receive clear answers to specific requests that will help us grow our faith.

Why do I point that out? Sometimes when we go to pray, we are afraid to pray. Instead, we say, "Lord bless this and bless him or her." It's only when we pray specifically that God answers specifically. Only then is our faith encouraged and strengthened. Sometimes we pray for the exact amount of money we need. At other times we pray for a specific job, relationship, deliverance, or healing, and when God answers specifically, we are encouraged that prayer is real because God is listening.

David asked if he should attack the Philistines. The Lord directed him to attack and save Keilah. David's men, however, were not so sure. They were already in a dangerous situation and David was proposing to put them in even more danger. David went back again to the Lord to make sure because he realized it wasn't just him going but a whole army of men. Once again, God told him to proceed to Keilah.

God answered clearly. Some Christians wish God would speak to them that way today. God has not lost His ability to communicate and He can speak audibly if He so chooses. Sometimes God speaks louder than when He is speaking out loud. There were times when our parents only had a look at us and it was as if they shouted. Not a word needed to be said but the eye contact made us rehearse everything that was going to happen to us if we proceeded on our intended course of action.

God doesn't always have to speak out loud. He primarily speaks through His word and by His Spirit. If we would learn to pray in accordance with the will of God, we would actually hear God answer us specifically and clearly. If we are not praying specifically according to the will of God, it's just an exercise in futility. John wrote in one of his epistles,

> These things I have written to you who believe in the name of the Son of God, that you may know that you have eternal life, and that you may continue to believe in the name of the Son of God (1 John 5:13).

We must realize beyond a shadow of a doubt that we possess eternal life, that the life of God is permanently invested in us. His life has merged with our being. The reason John wrote was so we could have absolute assurance that we have eternal life so we would continue to believe in the name of the son of God.

John went on to say the name represents all the person is and all they stand for. When we say the name of the son of God, we identify with all He has done. He is God manifested in the flesh, who died for us and rose again on the third day, who justified us in the sight of God forever and ever lives to make intercession for us. Believe in who He is and in all that He has done for you.

14 Now this is the confidence that we have in Him, that if we ask anything according to His will, He hears us. 15 And if we know that He hears us, whatever we ask, we know that we have the petitions that we have asked of Him (1 John 5:14-15).

This is the confidence we should have in God that if we ask anything in accordance with his will, He hears us. Likewise, it means if we are praying and it is not in accordance with His will, He hears the noise coming out of our mouths and recognizes our voice, but He doesn't hear us. If he hears you, it means you prayed in accordance with His will, whatever it was you asked as verse 15 assures us.

The problem is that the manifestation of that reality doesn't happen right away. You pray in accordance with His will, but you want to see it come to pass in the next five minutes. It may be 15 years before you are ready to have what God gave you. Parents should set aside money for their children when they are young. They are not going to get that money now because they would blow it at a candy store. They will need it whenever they go to college. but it's already there for them. God is saying if we would pray in accordance with His will, He will hear that prayer and answer. We would have it now.

That lets me know a lot of the prayers we pray are simply not in accordance with God's will for us. We usually know what we want for ourselves, but we're not that interested in what God may want for us. That's not the thing we are praying for. We are still on the throne and aren't pursuing His kingdom—it's still "my" kingdom.

GOD STILL SPEAKS TO HIS PEOPLE

God knows what and who we need. He knows who He planned for us to be with and that's how we need to pray. David was hearing from God to go to the people of Keilah. God had his back and would give him the victory. It says in verse six that one of the priests who came with David, Abiathar, had his ephod with him. God designed clothing for the priests to wear. The ephod was a breastplate and it had stones that represented all the tribes. Sometimes that garment was referred to as the Urim and the Thummin. When the priest prayed to discover God's will, He would cause the lights of the stones on the breastplates to light up or not light up and so they could know what God was saying in response to their petition.

Christians sometimes wish God would speak to them like he did to Abraham and David, or to the priests who wore the ephod. Some wish He would send fire like He once did. Don't we realize we have the Spirit of God living in us? We also have the completed canon of Scripture in our hands. God has said so much to us that we haven't cared enough to read about or heed yet, so why should He say anything else? The reason some of us don't hear from God is that we're saying, "I really don't care what You have already said to me, even though You have made it clear that this is what I need to live my best life." God is saying, "If you don't care what I've already said to you, what makes you think I am going to jump now when you want an answer?"

There is recorded in His word everything we need to live our lives. I know some believers who have known the Lord a long time and have not read through the Bible. They read seven or eight books every school semester. They watch countless hours of television every day. God gave them one book describing how much He loves them and how to live life victoriously and they don't want to study or read it.

God is speaking but we are not listening. If we show that we care enough to listen to what He says, I promise we will hear Him more and more. We will receive more direction, clarity, and timely information if we pay the price and study the word of God. The enemy is not going to oppose you when you are flipping television channels. He's not going to attack you if you hang out with your friends. Whenever you study the Word, however, there will be opposition and distractions from all over the place. You must push through all that.

Jesus made it clear in John 10 that His sheep know His voice. They listen to and follow Him and won't follow the voice of anyone else. If you are one of His sheep, you will be able to discern the voice of your Shepherd. In Acts 22, Paul shared his conversion testimony of when God called him out of darkness and into the light as he persecuted the church.

> 6 "Now it happened, as I journeyed and came near Damascus at about noon, suddenly a great light from

heaven shone around me. [7] And I fell to the ground and heard a voice saying to me, 'Saul, Saul, why are you persecuting Me?' [8] So I answered, 'Who are You, Lord?' And He said to me, 'I am Jesus of Nazareth, whom you are persecuting.' [9] "And those who were with me indeed saw the light and were afraid, but they did not hear the voice of Him who spoke to me" (Acts 22:6-9).

When you read the other accounts of this testimony, they state that everybody heard a noise but only Saul heard clearly what God was saying. If you are His child, you can clearly hear and discern what He is saying directly to you.

[9] "And those who were with me indeed saw the light and were afraid, but they did not hear the voice of Him who spoke to me. [10] So I said, 'What shall I do, Lord?' And the Lord said to me, 'Arise and go into Damascus, and there you will be told all things which are appointed for you to do.' [11] And since I could not see for the glory of that light, being led by the hand of those who were with me, I came into Damascus. [12] "Then a certain Ananias, a devout man according to the law, having a good testimony with all the Jews who dwelt there, [13] came to me; and he stood and said to me, 'Brother Saul, that had to be something to hear that, knowing that he was a persecutor of the church. Brother Saul Receive your sight.' And at that same hour I looked up at him. [14] Then he said, 'The God of our fathers has chosen you that you should know His will, and see the Just One'" (Acts 22:9-14).

That's not how it was only for Paul. If God has chosen to save you, He has given you the privilege of knowing and understanding who Jesus Christ is and the privilege of hearing Him speak to you. There is a world full of people who are walking around lost because they don't recognize the voice of God. Jesus said if we are His, we have the privilege of hearing and discerning His voice that can guide us through every step of life.

Many believers have an advantage they seldom use. They choose to rely on self-centered logic like Saul did, instead of supernatural communication like David. The story continues in 1 Samuel 23:7:

> [7] And Saul was told that David had gone to Keilah. So Saul said, "God has delivered him into my hand, for he has shut himself in by entering a town that has gates and bars." [8] Then Saul called all the people together for war, to go down to Keilah to besiege David and his men. [9] When David knew that Saul plotted evil against him, he said to Abiathar the priest, "Bring the ephod here." [10] Then David said, "O Lord God of Israel, Your servant has certainly heard that Saul seeks to come to Keilah to destroy the city for my sake. [11] Will the men of Keilah deliver me into his hand? Will Saul come down, as Your servant has heard? O Lord God of Israel, I pray, tell Your servant." And the Lord said, "He will come down." [12] Then David said, "Will the men of Keilah deliver me and my men into the hand of Saul? "And the Lord said, "They will deliver you." [13] So David and his men, about six hundred, arose and departed from Keilah and went wherever they could go. Then it was told Saul that David had escaped from Keilah; so he halted the expedition (1 Samuel 23:7-13).

Saul is so deceived at this point that when he heard David was in Keilah defending Israelites who Saul should have been defending, he saw it as an answer to prayer. David was trapped and Saul believed he had him. David asked more specific questions like, "Is Saul coming here to get me. Are these people who I just rescued going to turn me into Saul?" We would hope they would not do that—but they did. In the last chapter, we read how Saul thought the priests had conspired with David against him and had them slaughtered. Saul was then concerned that the Keilah inhabitants were going to be loyal to David instead of to him, even though they had good reason due to David's rescue.

God warned David that the residents were going to turn him in. David was getting supernatural communication from the Lord and Saul was depending on human logic. In the same way God revealed to David the entrapments of Saul, we need to depend upon our communication with the Lord to avoid the snares of Satan and his demons. Do you realize if you're a child of God on a mission from God, the enemy is regularly laying traps for you? If you're not reading the word of God and praying, you're going to walk right into one of those traps. When you pray, God will tell you what you need to know.

If you are about His business, if you care about His kingdom instead of your own, He will talk to you. Many of the psalms that have blessed us were written by David while he was being hunted down by Saul. He wrote those psalms because God kept delivering him from his enemies. Let's get to look at two of them:

> [1] Be merciful to me, O God, be merciful to me! For my soul trusts in You; And in the shadow of Your wings I will make my refuge, Until these calamities have passed by. [2] I will cry out to God Most High, to God who performs all things for me. [3] He shall send from heaven and save me; He reproaches the one who would swallow me up. Selah God shall send forth His mercy and His truth. [4] My soul is among lions; I lie among the sons of men Who are set on fire, Whose teeth are spears and arrows, And their tongue a sharp sword. [5] Be exalted, O God, above the heavens; Let Your glory be above all the earth (Psalm 57:1-5).

Psalm 27 may be one you are more familiar with:

> [1] The Lord is my light and my salvation; Whom shall I fear? The Lord is the strength of my life; Of whom shall I be afraid? [2] When the wicked came against me to eat up my flesh, My enemies and foes, They stumbled and fell. [3] Though an army may encamp against me, My heart shall not fear; Though war may rise against me, In this I will be confident. [4] One thing I have desired of the Lord, That will I seek: That I may dwell in the house of the Lord All the days of my life, to behold the beauty of the Lord, And to inquire in His temple. [5] For in the time of trouble He shall hide me in His pavilion; In the secret place of His tabernacle He shall hide me; He shall set me high upon a rock (Psalm 27:1-5).

David was writing psalms from his life experience because God delivered him again and again. He delivered him from people who were plotting to take his life. You'll see these psalms differently when you have gone through something similar. You may hear the same words of a psalm you have heard all your life, but when God has raised you off a deathbed, or brought you out of financial trouble, or healed a relationship you had given up on, you will sing and read those psalms differently.

I used to sing *Amazing Grace* before I experienced that grace or realized how much I needed it. You should be singing that song all the days of your eternal life. *Amazing grace, how sweet the sound, that saved a wretch like me.* Sometimes this is what we are thinking when we sing it. *God, You are great! You saved all those wicked horrible friends of mine. I didn't need that much grace, God. You know how good I am. I know the song says a wretch like me, but I'm really no wretch.*

David knew what it was like to be overwhelmed by amazing grace. There is no way he would have gotten away from Saul on his own except that God spared him. Saul thought God was giving David into his hands, but the opposite was true. He was keeping David out of Saul's hands.

The Lord speaks to us in various ways today, but always in alignment with what Scripture has revealed about His nature, purposes, and plans. He frequently uses His saints to encourage and remind us of His promises.

DAVID HIDES IN THE WILDERNESS

In the midst of being chased and persecuted, along came David's good friend Jonathan. He knew his father was off the hook and crazy. He knew that David was God's chosen and he had been interceding, trying to help and protect his good friend from his crazy father.

> [14] And David stayed in strongholds in the wilderness, and remained in the mountains in the Wilderness of Ziph. Saul sought him every day, but God did not deliver him into his hand. [15] So David saw that Saul had come out to seek his life. And David was in the Wilderness of Ziph in a forest. [16] Then Jonathan, Saul's son, arose and went to David in the woods and strengthened his hand in God (1 Samuel 23:14-16).

God kept Saul from capturing David but let Jonathan get to him so he could encourage him, and then we read, "And he [Jonathan] said to him, 'Do not fear, for the hand of Saul my father shall not find you. You shall be king over Israel, and I shall be next to you. Even my father Saul knows that'" (1 Samuel 23:17).

Jonathan said even though Saul was trying to kill David, Saul realized David was going to be king. Saul was only trying to make his life miserable, but he knew the end of this movie was already written. It's amazing what people do when they know that they don't even have a chance. They refuse to surrender their way of doing things, refuse to surrender the throne of their lives. "So the two of them made a covenant before the Lord. And David stayed in the woods, and Jonathan went to his own house" (1 Samuel 23:18).

Throughout chapter 23, David continued to hide. Some scholars tell us that these were huge caves carved into rocks in which 50,000 people could have been hiding. That helps us understand how David and Saul could have been in the same cave but not really see one another. Saul continued to pursue David and we read near the end of chapter 23,

> 21 And Saul said, "Blessed are you of the Lord, for you have compassion on me. 22 Please go and find out for sure, and see the place where his hideout is, and who has seen him there. For I am told he is very crafty. 23 See therefore, and take knowledge of all the lurking places where he hides; and come back to me with certainty, and I will go with you. And it shall be, if he is in the land, that I will search for him throughout all the clans of Judah." 24 So they arose and went to Ziph before Saul. But David and his men were in the Wilderness of Maon, in the plain on the south of Jeshimon. 25 When Saul and his men went to seek him, they told David. Therefore he went down to the rock, and stayed in the Wilderness of Maon. And when Saul heard that, he pursued David in the Wilderness of Maon. 23 Then Saul went on one side of the mountain, and David and his men on the other side of the mountain. So David made haste to get away from Saul, for Saul and

his men were encircling David and his men to take them. [27] But a messenger came to Saul, saying, "Hurry and come, for the Philistines have invaded the land!" [28] Therefore Saul returned from pursuing David, and went against the Philistines; so they called that place the Rock of Escape. [29] Then David went up from there and dwelt in strongholds at En Gedi (1 Samuel 23:21-29).

Picture David going around the mountains and then all of a sudden they say, "Saul! The Philistines our real enemy are here. They are destroying our land. You had better come fight the battle you should have been fighting in the first place." God used that to get Saul away from David for a time. God never runs out of ways to protect His people.

Some people claim to speak on behalf of the Lord, but they are simply using His name for selfish purposes and without the authority to do so. Trust God to help you distinguish between the true messenger and a religious manipulator. Saul kept thinking God was answering his prayers. He kept telling people the Lord was going to bless them for helping him. Saul knew how to use God's name just like people in pulpits and on television today who use the name of God and say, "God is going to bless you abundantly, *if* you sow some seed money into this ministry. If you put $1,000 into this ministry, I promise you by this time next year, you're going to have $100,000 in return." People listen and write the checks!

DAVID MEETS SAUL

In Chapter 24, we see that the Lord may deliver your enemies into your hand but that doesn't mean you have permission to treat them like they treat you. Grace provides the atmosphere that makes repentance possible. Some of you may not want to look at this chapter because you are driven by adrenaline from the thought of getting even with the people who hurt you. God may want you to show them some grace, perhaps the same grace you needed at one time.

[1] Now it happened, when Saul had returned from following the Philistines, that it was told him, saying,

"Take note! David is in the Wilderness of En Gedi."
[2] Then Saul took three thousand chosen men from all Israel, and went to seek David and his men on the Rocks of the Wild Goats (1 Samuel 24:1-2).

Let that sink in. The king of Israel who should have been focused on protecting the Israelites from the Philistines and other enemies took 3,000 men with him to pursue his son-in-law, one of his mightiest soldiers who had protected him, killed a lion with his hands, and who sang a song of praise whenever the demons had turned Saul upside down. Saul took all those soldiers just so he could go after David and his crew. Saul was out of his mind with jealousy and envy.

God records those things in the Bible so we can learn the danger of being jealous and envious of what God has done for others. God will give you everything you need if you do His will. Don't do it because you want what you want or to get what others have.

"So he came to the sheepfolds by the road, where there was a cave; and Saul went in to attend to his needs. (David and his men were staying in the recesses of the cave.)" (1 Samuel 24:3). The King James Bible states that Saul went in to cover his feet. The New King James says he went in to attend to his needs. My translation is he wanted to use the bathroom. Saul wore a robe and when he had to do his business, he covered his feet. After he relieved himself, he rested and fell asleep. Then we see another surprising answer to prayer:

[4] Then the men of David said to him, "This is the day of which the Lord said to you, 'Behold, I will deliver your enemy into your hand, that you may do to him as it seems good to you.'" And David arose and secretly cut off a corner of Saul's robe. [5] Now it happened afterward that David's heart troubled him because he had cut Saul's robe. [6] And he said to his men, "The Lord forbid that I should do this thing to my master, the Lord's anointed, to stretch out my hand against him, seeing he is the anointed of the Lord" (1 Samuel 24:4-6).

David's 600-plus men were protecting him while running

from Saul at the same time. They thought their prayers were answered and God had delivered their enemy into their hand. They advised David, "You can kill him, and we can all go back to our families." Instead, what did David do? He snuck up to Saul and cut off the back corner of his kingly robe without Saul knowing. He didn't do any harm to Saul and then he was convicted that he should not have even done that to him.

It takes the Spirit of God to prevent us from seeking vengeance or getting even, sometimes going beyond an eye for an eye. Victory comes when we show Christ in us rather than normal fleshly responses. David knew God had put Saul in this position, but God did not tell him to kill the king. He decided he wasn't going to touch him.

Many preachers love this passage because they interpret it to mean no one is supposed to touch the anointed of God. That is an incorrect application, and we must tell the story the way God wrote it and only then can we make the proper application. Saul was not the best example in the Bible of an anointed person, but David recognized that God didn't give him permission to take him out. He cut off his robe but didn't hurt him. It took the supernatural restraint of God to keep him from getting even.

It took me years to understand why God said in Exodus 21 "an eye for an eye and a tooth for tooth, a foot for a foot." Why did he say that? If a bully on your street knocks out your little daughter's tooth, when you get your hands on him or her, are you going to knock out one tooth or are you going to knock out all of them so the person needs dentures? Of course, that's not the way to handle the problem, but you get my point. We would be angry and want to inflict more damage on the bully than he or she inflicted on our loved one. God was directing His people to only get back the equal damage that was done to them. The godliest person reading this book could have a hard time only going that far with an injustice.

If somebody hits your car that's worth $1,000 and you want to sue for $50,000, you are only entitled to what you lost! I want $100,000 for emotional damage added. We are out of control without the Holy Spirit. God restrained David because he could have killed him, but he did not.

⁸ David also arose afterward, went out of the cave, and

called out to Saul, saying, "My lord the king!" And when Saul looked behind him, David stooped with his face to the earth, and bowed down. [9] And David said to Saul: "Why do you listen to the words of men who say, 'Indeed David seeks your harm'? [10] Look, this day your eyes have seen that the Lord delivered you today into my hand in the cave, and someone urged me to kill you. But my eye spared you, and I said, 'I will not stretch out my hand against my lord, for he is the Lord's anointed.' [11] Moreover, my father, see! Yes, see the corner of your robe in my hand! For in that I cut off the corner of your robe, and did not kill you, know and see that there is neither evil nor rebellion in my hand, and I have not sinned against you. Yet you hunt my life to take it. [12] Let the Lord judge between you and me, and let the Lord avenge me on you. But my hand shall not be against you. [13] As the proverb of the ancients says, 'Wickedness proceeds from the wicked.' But my hand shall not be against you. [14] After whom has the king of Israel come out? Whom do you pursue? A dead dog? A flea? [15] Therefore let the Lord be judge, and judge between you and me, and see and plead my case, and deliver me out of your hand" (1 Samuel 24:8-15).

You see David's humility in this passage. He could have killed Saul, but he told him he didn't along with the reason why. He urged Saul not to listen to his advisors who were saying David was trying to harm him. He reminded Saul he was there to serve him. When we know God has given us something, we don't have to be jealous or hurt anybody else. David understood that God had called him to be king one day. He didn't have to push Saul out of the way to get to the throne. He determined to serve Saul until David's time came.

We see what God can do in a human life when that person waits their turn. We don't have to be jealous and envious of what other people have. We only need to praise God for what we have. God can give everybody everything they need. Doesn't the psalm say he opens His hand and satisfies the needs of every living creature that he has created? (see Psalm 145:16). I can open my wallet and maybe help two or three people. God says He can open up His hand and satisfy every creature He created. He has that much power.

David asked Saul why he was chasing him, asking if he was a dead dog? Dogs were not house pets then like they are today. They were street scavengers and flea bags. To call someone a dog was an insult in that cultural context. David claimed he was not a dog and asked why Saul was bringing thousands of men against him.

> [16] So it was, when David had finished speaking these words to Saul, that Saul said, "Is this your voice, my son David?" And Saul lifted up his voice and wept. [17] Then he said to David: "You are more righteous than I; for you have rewarded me with good, whereas I have rewarded you with evil. [18] And you have shown this day how you have dealt well with me; for when the Lord delivered me into your hand, you did not kill me. [19] For if a man finds his enemy, will he let him get away safely? Therefore may the Lord reward you with good for what you have done to me this day. [20] And now I know indeed that you shall surely be king, and that the kingdom of Israel shall be established in your hand. [21] Therefore swear now to me by the Lord that you will not cut off my descendants after me, and that you will not destroy my name from my father's house." [22] So David swore to Saul. And Saul went home, but David and his men went up to the stronghold (1 Samuel 24:16-22).

Saul was convicted but it didn't lead to repentance. If you read the rest of 1 Samuel, you see that this is not the end of the story. Saul came after David again. Conviction is important, but it doesn't always lead to repentance. He said all the right things in 1 Samuel 24. Don't be fooled by words that are not followed up with lifestyle changes. The abuser often says the right words: "Oh I'm sorry. I didn't mean to hurt you. I'll never do that again— until my next opportunity!"

People can be convicted but they don't repent. Until there is true repentance, the behavior is not going to change. Have you been in a church when somebody comes forward every three or four weeks? They come up crying, drowning the altar with their tears, but the next week they are back out doing the same thing. They were convicted but they didn't allow the Spirit of God to lead them all the way to repentance, which leads to a change of mind and then to a change of action never to return. Even Judas seemed sorry after he had messed up and betrayed Jesus. He didn't repent and went out and took his life.

Self-serving sorrow and remorse are not repentance. Saul was convicted but his heart was still not changed. Look in the mirror. Are you still doing the same things you have been convicted of again and again? If so, you have not repented.

In summary, God speaks clearly and answers prayer. The Lord always answers prayer in accordance with His will. He speaks better than we listen. Learn to communicate with Him; He will guide you through every step of your life. Pray with me, won't you?

> *Thank you, Lord, for the reminder of the power of prayer, and how important it is to pray specifically and in alignment with Your will. We confess that we do not always pray in faith, believing that You have promised to answer every prayer in accord with Your will. We pray You remind those persons who long for the days when You answered prayers audibly and often in clear demonstrations of power that You are still the God who speaks and acts. Help us understand that You can speak loudly without speaking audibly as Your Spirit communes with ours. Remind us that You want us to know Your will even more than we want to know it, and that as we stay close to You, we will discover that Your will is always good, acceptable, and perfect for us. With thanksgiving and praise we pray, amen.*

LEAVE VENGEANCE
TO THE LORD

Anita and I were walking together recently. She likes to walk for exercise. I'd rather drive. Sometimes a man just has to give in. We were reflecting on a time many years ago when I wasn't as mature as I am now when she was in Columbus and I was in Cleveland. There was a man who was harassing her and damaging her car and I feared for her safety. I asked permission to leave my job and I had no business or right to do so, but I told my boss and he didn't fire me. I'm so glad God did not let me see that person, for Lord only knows what might have happened. I probably would not be preaching today. It was an issue that blew over, but the enemy was baiting a trap and I almost fell into it. It was only because of the grace of God that nothing went horribly wrong that day.

I'm sure all of us have stories where in the moment we thought we were about to do the right thing, but it would have been tragic. Then we read the word of God and we see that God says, "Let me handle the vengeance part." God knows how to settle the score much better than we do. We know what might make us feel good in a moment of retaliation, but what about after the satisfaction of the moment? What if our way of getting even interferes with what God wants to accomplish with His plan?

We left off in the last chapter learning how David graciously spared Saul's life. First Samuel 25 relates what Saul did after he had said all the right words, but his heart had not changed. David was not through running from Saul. Chapter 25 starts out with a verse that seems to come out of nowhere: "Then Samuel died; and the Israelites gathered together and lamented for him and buried him at his home in Ramah. And David arose and went down to the Wilderness of Paran" (1 Samuel 25:1).

We all need to recognize the importance of those people

who support us and keep us emotionally balanced. There is a reason the Holy Spirit lets us see here that Samuel had died and David went down to the wilderness while all of Israel mourned. David had always been able to count on Samuel for spiritual guidance and emotional support. His death was a huge loss at a difficult time in David's life. Once again, he was fugitive on the run, and his go-to man was gone.

Stop and think what kind of legacy you are leaving. How many lives will be deeply be impacted by the fact that you are no longer here? Samuel had that kind of impact on people's lives. His family had not been there for David but Samuel was. Saul was trying to kill him but Samuel was praying for and supporting him. David was grieving, alone, and separated from his good friend Jonathan. In those moments when all human support seems to be absent, it is helpful to remember that our Lord went through similar times and taught us the Father never leaves us alone (see Mark 14:37 and John 16:32).

Nabal the Fool

[2] Now there was a man in Maon whose business was in Carmel, and the man was very rich. He had three thousand sheep and a thousand goats. And he was shearing his sheep in Carmel. [3] The name of the man was Nabal, and the name of his wife Abigail. And she was a woman of good understanding and beautiful appearance; but the man was harsh and evil in his doings. He was of the house of Caleb.

[4] When David heard in the wilderness that Nabal was shearing his sheep, [5] David sent ten young men; and David said to the young men, "Go up to Carmel, go to Nabal, and greet him in my name. [6] And thus you shall say to him who lives in prosperity: 'Peace be to you, peace to your house, and peace to all that you have! [7] Now I have heard that you have shearers. Your shepherds were with us, and we did not hurt them, nor was there anything missing from them all the while they were in Carmel. [8] Ask your young men, and they will tell you. Therefore let my young men

find favor in your eyes, for we come on a feast day. Please give whatever comes to your hand to your servants and to your son David.'" ⁹ So when David's young men came, they spoke to Nabal according to all these words in the name of David, and waited (1 Samuel 25:2-9).

We will be disappointed if we expect people to give us an equal return on our investment in them. We should rejoice with those who do and not overreact to those who don't.

Nabal was a wealthy man who possessed thousands of sheep. It was time to shear their wool to sell and outlaws would try to steal the wool headed for market. Just as David served to protect Keilah, he and his men were protecting Nabal along with his servants and business. David had his men approach Nabal for some type of payment in the form of provisions for his men in return for their protection. They did not seize what belonged to Nabal but politely and respectfully asked. The future king was approaching one of his future subjects but doing it with honor and dignity. To David's surprise, Nabal not only refused, he refused rudely and with disrespect: "Nabal's answered David servants and said, 'Who is David? Who is the son of Jesse?'" (1 Samuel 25:10).

What he said revealed that Nabal knew exactly who David was—the son of Jesse. He knew he was a military hero who was chosen to be the next king, yet he showed nothing but utter contempt for David. Nabal claimed there were many servants who were breaking away from their masters. He said David was a rebel, a fugitive, and lawbreaker.

¹¹ "Shall I then take my bread and my water and my meat that I have killed for my shearers, and give it to men when I do not know where they are from?" ¹² So David's young men turned on their heels and went back; and they came and told him all these words. ¹³ Then David said to his men, "Every man gird on his sword." So every man girded on his sword, and David also girded on his sword. And about four hundred men went with David, and two hundred stayed with the supplies (1 Samuel 25:11-13).

David had had enough disrespect, and he overreacted to

Nabal's insult. This is the same man who dodged Saul's spears and had been chased in the wilderness, but still showed grace to Saul. After this one offense, David was ready to lock and load and kill. We must be in touch with who we are spilling over on to. A lot of times we are dumping our anger, frustration, and disappointment on the people who really didn't put us in that position. They just happen to be in our lives at the moment to receive what's going on inside of us. We can catch ourselves being annoyed and irritable, which we skillfully hide from others, but we feel it inside ourselves. Those feelings come from a long line of things that didn't happen at that moment but happened and accumulated before that moment. We must be careful not to react out of frustration when people we pour into do not give us the expected return on our investment in them.

My wife and I recently celebrated our 23rd anniversary at the church we planted and serve. I can't tell you how many people have come in and out of our doors, probably a couple of thousand. We invested in a lot of those people. Some came when they were hurting and were in need and as soon as they got what they wanted, they were gone without even a goodbye or a forwarding address. When that happened, it would be easy to stop giving to those who need us to give to them because we think they represent another disappointment waiting to happen.

Jesus knows how we feel because He has done much more than that for billions of people. Every once in a while, one of them says thank you, as symbolized by the story of the ten lepers in Luke 17:11-19. We have to be careful not to overreact when we're disappointed. Some people can't love us because they have been hurt so many times in the past and have not yet learned how to let the Lord heal their souls. That person may be the one God put in your life to facilitate your healing journey as you seek to minister to them. Don't take it out on them. As one writer said, we are all wounded healers as we serve the Lord. David was in such an emotional hole, however, that he was ready to kill Nabal, and not just Nabal but all those around him.

ABIGAIL THE WISE

14 Now one of the young men told Abigail, Nabal's wife, saying, "Look, David sent messengers from the

wilderness to greet our master; and he reviled them. [15] But the men were very good to us, and we were not hurt, nor did we miss anything as long as we accompanied them, when we were in the fields. [16] They were a wall to us both by night and day, all the time we were with them keeping the sheep. [17] Now therefore, know and consider what you will do, for harm is determined against our master and against all his household. For he is such a scoundrel that one cannot speak to him" (1 Samuel 25:14-17).

Nabal's name meant folly or fool. Parents need to be careful what they name their children or when they assign nicknames. Sometimes they will live down to our expectations and other times we may crush them with the words we say to them. "You're stupid. You're worthless. You're ugly. We prayed for a girl and God gave us you." I have known successful adult men who said their father told them they would never amount to anything. They were in their fifties or sixties and they still felt like failures because those words had taken root in their souls.

I don't know where Nabal got his name or his nickname but he lived up to it, for he was a foolish man. When one of the servants came to his wife, Abigail, to say that her husband was a fool, she did not seem surprised or offended. They reported to Abigail that her husband was about to get them all killed. Abigail was a fine example of how to draw upon grace and wisdom to deal with a difficult marriage partner. She did not have the marriage she wanted but she had the grace and wisdom from God that she needed.

It's easy to focus on what we don't have instead of listening to God's voice in our lives telling us we have all we need to handle whatever situation He has allowed us to be in. She knew she was married to somebody who was difficult to deal with. The Bible tells us that she was intelligent and wise, a woman of understanding, and beautiful. All that was said about her husband was that he was foolish. He had money but he was a fool. Money and wisdom don't always go together.

The servants appealed to Abigail for help. First Samuel chapter 25 describes an incredible lady doing a lot of good intercessory work. She realized there were hundreds of hungry, angry men on their way. She set herself to work but did not tell her husband.

> [18] Then Abigail made haste and took two hundred loaves of bread, two skins of wine, five sheep already dressed, five seahs of roasted grain, one hundred clusters of raisins, and two hundred cakes of figs, and loaded them on donkeys. [19] And she said to her servants, "Go on before me; see, I am coming after you." But she did not tell her husband Nabal (1 Samuel 25:18-19.

As it was, she rode on a donkey and went down under cover of the hill. Suddenly there were David and his men, coming down toward her, and she met them. That's the providence of God. She got there just at the right time with food before David could get to Nabal.

> [21] Now David had said, "Surely in vain I have protected all that this fellow has in the wilderness, so that nothing was missed of all that belongs to him. And he has repaid me evil for good. [22] May God do so, and more also, to the enemies of David, if I leave one male of all who belong to him by morning light."
>
> [23] Now when Abigail saw David, she dismounted quickly from the donkey, fell on her face before David, and bowed down to the ground. [24] So she fell at his feet and said: "On me, my lord, on me let this iniquity be! And please let your maidservant speak in your ears, and hear the words of your maidservant. [25] Please, let not my lord regard this scoundrel Nabal. For as his name is, so is he: Nabal is his name, and folly is with him! But I, your maidservant, did not see the young men of my lord whom you sent. [26] Now therefore, my lord, as the Lord lives and as your soul lives, since the Lord has held you back from coming to bloodshed and from avenging yourself with your own hand, now then, let your enemies and those who seek harm for my lord be as Nabal. [27] And now this present which your maidservant has brought to my lord, let it be given to the young men who follow my lord. [28] Please

forgive the trespass of your maidservant. For the Lord will certainly make for my lord an enduring house, because my lord fights the battles of the Lord, and evil is not found in you throughout your days" (1 Samuel 25:21-28).

The word *lord* she used basically meant *sir.* She was being respectful to him. She took the blame upon herself even though she was not involved in Nabal's actions. She took ownership of it to diffuse the situation. Abigail was interceding, calming this angry man's spirit. Abigail presented what David had asked for, and reminded David of what the Lord Jehovah had promised to do through him, urging him not to throw that away in a moment of vengeance.

"Yet a man has risen to pursue you and seek your life, but the life of my lord shall be bound in the bundle of the living with the Lord your God; and the lives of your enemies He shall sling out, as from the pocket of a sling" (1 Samuel 25:29).

Doesn't that remind you of the sling David used whenever he slew Goliath? I am sure it brought that to David's mind as well.

30 And it shall come to pass, when the Lord has done for my lord according to all the good that He has spoken concerning you, and has appointed you ruler over Israel, 31 that this will be no grief to you, nor offense of heart to my lord, either that you have shed blood without cause, or that my lord has avenged himself. But when the Lord has dealt well with my lord, then remember your maidservant" (1 Samuel 25:30-31).

That was a wise woman!

32 Then David said to Abigail: "Blessed is the Lord God of Israel, who sent you this day to meet me! 33 And blessed is your advice and blessed are you, because you have kept me this day from coming to bloodshed and from avenging myself with my own hand. 34 For indeed, as the Lord God of Israel lives, who has kept me back from hurting you, unless you had hurried and

come to meet me, surely by morning light no males would have been left to Nabal!" (1 Samuel 25:32-34).

David realized that God sent Abigail to him. He admitted he was so angry that if she had not arrived, he was going to kill her husband and everybody else who worked for him. We can all say, "Thank You, Jesus, for stopping me from doing what I felt like doing in a moment of rage, anger, disappointment, or frustration. I would have had a lifetime of regrets." David didn't get what he wanted from Nabal but he got what he needed from the Lord.

Luke 6 gave us directives about what we should do when we are insulted, slighted, or provoked. God is not saying to be a punching bag. When we give expecting nothing in return, we will always blessed by the spiritual return on our investments. Let's look at the part of the Scripture in Luke that some of the prosperity preachers don't focus and then parts that they do. God is a God of balance. That makes some things look like flat out contradictions, but we have to study and examine them in context:

> [27] "But I say to you who hear: Love your enemies, do good to those who hate you, [28] bless those who curse you, and pray for those who spitefully use you. [29] To him who strikes you on the one cheek, offer the other also. And from him, who takes away your cloak, do not withhold your tunic either. [30] Give to everyone who asks of you. And from him who takes away your goods do not ask them back. [31] And just as you want men to do to you, you also do to them likewise.

> [32] "But if you love those who love you, what credit is that to you? Credit there means grace. For even sinners love those who love them. [33] And if you do good to those who do good to you, what credit, what grace is that to you? For even sinners do the same. [34] And if you lend to those from whom you hope to receive back, what credit is that to you? For even sinners lend to sinners to receive as much back. [35] But love your enemies, do good, and lend, hoping for nothing in return" (Luke 6:27-35).

Sometimes as believers, we give because it's the right

thing to do. If we never see that money again, God bless and meet their needs and mine. Many of us say as we put the money in their hands, however, "God be with you till we meet again!" Sometimes God will pay you back, not through the one to whom you gave the money who you may never see again: [35] "And your reward will be great, and you will be sons of the Most High for He is kind to the unthankful and evil. [36] Therefore be merciful, just as your Father also is merciful" (Luke 6:35-36).

Here's the verse that is a favorite of the prosperity preachers: "Give and it will be given to you: good measure, pressed down, shaken together, and running over will be put into your bosom. For with the same measure that you use, it will be measured back to you" (Luke 6:38).

There are those wonderful times where you give and God gives you back a surprising return, more than you ever imagined. Then there are other times you will give, give, give, give, give, and give and you feel like there is absolutely nothing coming back from your investment. That is just the balance of Christianity. You are looking for your blessing from the east and it's coming from the west. You're looking for something to come back from the person you gave it to and God brings it back from ten other people. He gets it done, however He chooses, so we trust Him.

First Samuel chapter 25 ends with David acknowledging that Abigail had intervened and been a lifesaver, keeping him from doing something terribly wrong. Then something very interesting happened.

> [36] Now Abigail went to Nabal, and there he was, holding a feast in his house, like the feast of a king. And Nabal's heart was merry within him, for he was very drunk; therefore she told him nothing, little or much, until morning light. [37] So it was, in the morning, when the wine had gone from Nabal, and his wife had told him these things, that his heart died within him, and he became like a stone. [38] Then it happened, after about ten days, that the Lord struck Nabal, and he died (1 Samuel 25:36-38).

Now there is a danger when people preach from the Bible but they don't want to preach the Bible the way God wants it preached. They only want to find points of application, frequently taken out of context, for certain situations. This story is not indicating that Abigail wanted God to strike her husband down through a stroke or heart attack. That's not the proper application of this story.

God can deal with your spouse in whatever way He sees fit, but that does not mean you go home and pray, "Here I am, Lord, Abigail Jones. I'm tired of this fool, Lord. Will you take him out in Jesus' name?" The point is that God kept David from murdering a lot of innocent people but God took out Nabal so that did not have to be on David's conscience. The chapter ends with David marrying Abigail.

Scripture records the actions of its biblical characters without endorsing every decision they make. David made many choices that cost him dearly, yet the grace of God helped him praise his way through the consequences. For example, David had already been given a wife who Saul had given away to somebody else. First Samuel 25:43 says that he also took Ahinoam of Jezreel so both Abigail and Ahinoam were his wives. God never told him to take all those wives, but that's what he did. We read in 1 Chronicles 3:

> [1] Now these were the sons of David who were born to him in Hebron: The firstborn was Amnon, by Ahinoam the Jezreelitess; the second, Daniel, by Abigail the Carmelitess; [2] the third, Absalom the son of Maacah, the daughter of Talmai, king of Geshur; the fourth, Adonijah the son of Haggith; [3] the fifth, Shephatiah, by Abital; the sixth, Ithream, by his wife Eglah (1 Chronicles 3:1-3).

If we only read First Samuel, we don't know David took other wives and had other children and then it is difficult to see him as a godly man who was in pursuit of God's heart. He made some bad decisions motivated by lust and those came back to haunt him. Those relationships produced sons who would fight against one another, all wanting to be the next king. God reported what David did, but it never indicates God blessed or endorsed those actions. There are always consequences for violating the clear instructions of the Lord.

DAVID MEETS SAUL AGAIN

Let's take a quick at the last part of 1 Samuel 26. After David overreacted to Nabal, he had yet another interaction with Saul, being presented with another opportunity to take Saul out.

> [7] So David and Abishai came to the people by night; and there Saul lay sleeping within the camp, with his spear stuck in the ground by his head. And Abner and the people lay all around him. [8] Then Abishai said to David, "God has delivered your enemy into your hand this day. Now therefore, please, let me strike him at once with the spear, right to the earth; and I will not have to strike him a second time!" (1 Samuel 26:7-8).

David's men were once again at it, saying, "David, look! God has answered our prayers. Saul and his boys are asleep. The spear is right next to him. Take it and run him through just one time. Let me do it, David. I don't even have to stab him multiple times. One time and he's gone." As before, David resisted the temptation,

> [9] But David said to Abishai, "Do not destroy him; for who can stretch out his hand against the Lord's anointed, and be guiltless?" [10] David said furthermore, "As the Lord lives, the Lord shall strike him, or his day shall come to die, or he shall go out to battle and perish. [11] The Lord forbid that I should stretch out my hand against the Lord's anointed. But please, take now the spear and the jug of water that are by his head, and let us go." [12] So David took the spear and the jug of water by Saul's head, and they got away; and no man saw or knew it or awoke. For they were all asleep, because a deep sleep from the Lord had fallen on them (1 Samuel 26:9-12).

They could have awakened while David was approaching to take the weapons and it could have gotten ugly, but God had put them in a deep sleep so that didn't happen. When we read the rest of chapter 26, we learn that David went a distance away from the people before he called out to Abner, asking what kind of bodyguard he was. David was standing before them with the king's sword even though it had been Abner's job to protect him. David told Abner he could have killed him. Take note of that because later David and Abner have some issues and it goes back to this instance when David called him out. Once again Saul feels conviction without any real repentance.

> [21] Then Saul said, "I have sinned. Return, my son David, for I will harm you no more, because my life was precious in your eyes this day. Indeed I have played the fool and erred exceedingly." [22] And David answered and said, "Here is the king's spear. Let one of the young men come over and get it. [23] May the Lord repay every man for his righteousness and his faithfulness; for the Lord delivered you into my hand today, but I would not stretch out my hand against the Lord's anointed. [24] And indeed, as your life was valued much this day in my eyes, so let my life be valued much in the eyes of the Lord, and let Him deliver me out of all tribulation" (1 Samuel 26:21-24).

Abigail's words were still ringing in David's spirit after she told him that God was going to build and establish David a house. He was going to be king and his sons were going to succeed him. She said all that in the past tense because she had that kind of faith and understanding. She knew God's promise and David was realizing that God was going to bring it all to pass. In the next chapter, however, David was depressed because he still thought Saul was going to kill him.

When we are under stress all the time, we have emotional ups and downs. God brings us through something and we have victory but two days later, life is falling apart again and not even God can get us through it. *What's the point in all this?* We need to recognize all the dynamics that move us to make these decisions. We are saying things because we have not dealt with the stress, pressure, and disappointment. Then we start handling our relationships in horrible ways. David once again spared Saul.

God may want you to destroy your enemies by showing Christ-like love to them. Let His grace overwhelm your next reaction. We see that's what David did. Some people should be labeled EGR—extra grace required. They seldom keep their word and frequently cause us grief. Choose to allow Christ to show you how to deal with these recurring attacks because you forgive.

There are going to be people in your life and you, with all good biblical intentions, want to forgive them. You take all the biblical steps but as an emotional being, the feelings come back. You must rehearse and repeat your forgiveness again and again. Do that however many times it takes so you don't overreact and sin because of how you feel.

God may deliver our enemies into our hands, but He may command us to help rather than harm them. One of David's bodyguards said God had answered their prayers. David realized that God had answered their prayers by protecting them and keeping Saul from killing them. You need to know what your reaction is to be in every situation based on the Word of God and will of God for your life.

You can't love your enemies without the grace of God. Most of the time we struggle to love our friends, let alone our enemies. That really takes the love and grace of God flowing into and out of our hearts.

Forgiveness is a gift we all need. We receive a blessing every time we choose to share the gift we received from Christ. Set others free so you can experience freedom in the process. Forgiveness is not easy. God had to incarnate Himself, leave heaven, die on the cross, and rise from the dead to make forgiveness possible. It's not easy. In fact, it's impossible without the power of God flowing through our lives.

If we don't learn to forgive, we will be like David, ready to do harm to others over minor (or major) offenses, thus destroying relationships. And the sad part is it will be because of what somebody else did to us that we have not dealt with. If we do not receive forgiveness, we can't pass it on to someone.

If you are struggling in this area, maybe you have heard about the Lord, read about the Lord, come to church, given money, but never really received the life of Christ. I encourage you to surrender your life to the Lord, who will give you all the help you need to deal with every life situation you encounter.

*Father, as we reflect on how quickly we can let our
emotions get the best of us, we are even more grateful*

*for Your indwelling Holy Spirit, who makes it possible
for us to be under Your control rather than our own.
We pray You will continue to send people like Abigail
into our lives, and that we would listen to those persons
when they give us wise counsel.*

*Thank You for Your word that reminds us "not to
answer a fool according to his folly" and helps us speak
words of wisdom rather than return foolishness for
foolishness. Lord, guard us from taking vengeance into
our own hands in ways that dishonor You and teach us
to get out of Your way to let You handle those situations
for us. You always get it right, and we usually get it
wrong. Help us learn to value life just as You do. In the
name of our Lord Jesus Christ, we pray. Amen.*

FIRST SAMUEL 27-29

HEARING GOD IN DEPRESSION, DARKNESS, AND DECEPTION

In this chapter, let's look at hearing God's voice through depression, darkness, and deception. There are some things that sneak up on us and depress us for a second or two. I received something in the mail recently that said I was eligible to enroll for Medicare. I asked myself, *When did that happen? I was just enjoying being middle-aged a few days ago.*

Then I went into a fast-food place to grab a bite to eat. I had to look up at the menu and give them a number of the combo meal I wanted to order. The cashier said my order was $6, but I was always good at math and I knew that what I ordered was more than $7. I was going to be Christ-like and told her she had undercharged me, but then she explained she had given me a senior discount without asking my age. It was the first time in my life that had happened, and it forced me to deal with a new reality.

DAVID'S DEPRESSION

In the last chapter, we saw that God had once again spared David and all of his men from Saul's relentless pursuit. Saul had a moment of remorse for what he was trying to do and Jonathan showed up to encourage David. God reaffirmed to David that he would be the next king as He had frequently done, yet when we get to 1 Samuel 27, this is what we read:

> ¹ And David said in his heart, "Now I shall perish someday by the hand of Saul. There is nothing better for me than that I should speedily escape to the land of the Philistines; and Saul will despair of me, to seek me anymore in any part of Israel. So I shall escape out of his hand." ² Then David arose and went over with

the six hundred men who were with him to Achish the son of Maoch, king of Gath. ³ So David dwelt with Achish at Gath, he and his men, each man with his household, and David with his two wives, Ahinoam the Jezreelitess, and Abigail the Carmelitess, Nabal's widow. ⁴ And it was told Saul that David had fled to Gath; so he sought him no more (1 Samuel 27:1-4).

When we don't see a way out of depression, it affects our ability to hear the voice of God and to embrace His promises. We can read this passage and ask how David could come to this conclusion after God had spared him again and again while re-inforcing His promises to him. David heard and saw all God had done, but here he was declaring Saul was going to kill him some-day. He concluded he should run off to the land of the Philistines where maybe Saul would not find him, and he had a point, for Saul was doing anything but fight the enemies he should have been fighting. He spent all his time obsessed with trying to de-stroy David. When we get depressed and discouraged, even after a victory we can go right back into having a pity party fueled by unbiblical thinking. Despite God constantly delivering us and reminding us of His promises, we can assume everything is still going to go wrong.

It's not a sin to become depressed, but it is sinful to stay depressed. Everybody falls down, but if you choose to stay down, you have problems. Your physical fitness is manifested by how quickly you bounce back. If someone is in shape and runs 200 yards at their fastest pace, they're going to be gasping for breath when they cross the finish line. A short while later, that person will ge ready to run again. If you are in shape, you bounce back more quickly. If you are spiritually in shape, you bounce back from depression more quickly.

Sometimes we choose not to hear the voice of the Lord when we are discouraged. Let's look at a couple of thoughts di-rectly from David's pen. David wrote almost half of the psalms and some of them were written out of experiences he went through while God was maturing him.

Why do You stand afar off, O Lord? Why do You hide in times of trouble? Do you hear his heart? (Psalm 10:1).

¹ How long, O Lord? Will You forget me forever? How long will You hide Your face from me? ² How long shall I take counsel in my soul, Having sorrow in my heart daily? How long will my enemy be exalted over me? (Psalm 13:1-2).

Psalm 22 is what our Lord Jesus Christ quoted while He was on the cross:

¹ My God, My God, why have You forsaken Me? Why are You so far from helping Me, And from the words of My groaning? ² O My God, I cry in the daytime, but You do not hear; And in the night season, and am not silent (Psalm 22:1-2).

In 1 Samuel 27, we read some of the words that came out of David's heart while he was discouraged and depressed, seeking the Lord's precious voice while he was in an emotional valley. Keep in mind that this man had been hunted for years. Every day he woke up to the reality that the king of Israel, with thousands of men, was coming after him. He thought he was running out of hiding places. He had many men, with their wives and their children, to care for and think about. Assume each of them had a few children, which would mean David had a few thousand people for which he felt responsible.

He was their leader and all they knew was they were hiding and running, moving and hiding. David would not let them kill Saul so they could get on with their lives and return home. There are some great leadership lessons we can learn from this story. If we can keep people with us through things like that and they do not question our decision making, it means those people are committed. David cared for those people and was concerned about their provision. We can understand at that moment why he was discouraged. We all probably would have been feeling the same way.

The only way to keep your mind full of joy and peace is to remember the promises of God and what He has done for you in the past. He is a God who cannot lie. He keeps His word and promises to you. One preacher said that we should not forget in the dark what God taught us in the light, but we have a tendency to do that. Decisions made in depression without seeking God's face in prayer will lead us into unsafe spiritual, physical, and emotional places.

DAVID SEEKS PROTECTION
AMONG THE WICKED

David decided to hide in Philistia of all places. If the name Achish looks familiar, it's because he appeared a few chapters ago when David went to Philistia and acted like a madman before King Achish and the men of Gath. This is where he decided to go when he was depressed. This still wasn't a choice spot to take a vacation. Once you start down that slide by making those types of decisions, you wind up in places and wonder how you got there.

We read in 1 Samuel 27 that David said he was going to be loyal to the enemies of Israel: "Then David said to Achish, 'If I have now found favor in your eyes, let them give me a place in some town in the country, that I may dwell there. For why should your servant dwell in the royal city with you?'" (1 Samuel 27:5).

If I was to paraphrase, David was essentially saying, "King Achish, I don't deserve to live in your royal city. Just give me and my guys a little place in the projects so we can stay and we will serve you well." Achish gave them Ziklag that day. It is interesting to observe that Ziklag already belonged to Judah based upon Joshua 19:5, another fitting illustration of how often we fail to possess what the Lord has already given to us.

"Now the time that David dwelt in the country of the Philistines was one full year and four months" (1 Samuel 27:7). The rest of the chapter describes how David operated during that time, working as a double agent and destroying all living witnesses to his duplicitous lifestyle. While David pretended to battle for the Philistine king, he was actually going out to attack cities and areas controlled by the Philistines.

Because he could not leave an eyewitness to what he was doing, he had to murder every living thing and then come back and lie, telling the king of Philistia that they went to such and such a place and handled business in the king's best interests. King Achish was sure the Israelites would be so disgusted with David that he would have to serve with him forever.

That's a scary way to live because every day he had to wonder if he would be found out. If telling lies has become a lifestyle, it should be obvious you are not listening to the voice of God. You get yourself in a situation and all you can do is keep lying, hoping you won't be discovered.

At some point, you have to say, "Lord, I don't know how I got here, but I sure need your help to get out because I don't like living like this." God's voice can break through any situation we're in if we are willing to listen. The word of God is the only safe place for spiritual advice. All other sources, no matter how innocent or beneficial they appear to be, can be demonically informed.

> [1] Now it happened in those days that the Philistines gathered their armies together for war, to fight with Israel. And Achish said to David, "You assuredly know that you will go out with me to battle, you and your men." [2] So David said to Achish, "Surely you know what your servant can do." And Achish said to David, "Therefore I will make you one of my chief guardians forever" (1 Samuel 28:1-2).

The future king of Israel was promising to be a body-guard for the king of the Philistines. Isn't it amazing to see the situations we can wind up in when we are not in lockstep with the Holy Spirit? David continued to dig a hole for himself and his loyal followers, and there was no way out of this apart from the gracious intervention of the Lord Himself.

SAUL'S DESPERATION

The scenario then shifts back to Saul, who found himself in a desperate situation and in need of supernatural help. Not surprisingly, he again chose to disobey a clear directive from the Lord and still expected a good outcome.

> [3] Now Samuel had died, and all Israel had lamented for him and buried him in Ramah, in his own city. And Saul had put the mediums and the spiritists out of the land. [4] Then the Philistines gathered together, and came and encamped at Shunem. So Saul gathered all Israel together, and they encamped at Gilboa. [5] When Saul saw the army of the Philistines, he was afraid, and his heart trembled greatly. [6] And when Saul

inquired of the Lord, the Lord did not answer him, either by dreams or by Urim or by the prophets (1 Samuel 28:3-6).

As we discussed earlier, the high priest wore a breastplate with embedded stones representing the tribes of Israel. Urim (lights) and Thummin (perfections) were objects, generally believed to have a shiny side and a dull side, which were used to determine God's will in certain situations (see Exodus 28:30 and Numbers 27:21). God revealed His will at times by causing the stones to become brighter or less so, oftentimes indicating a yes or no answer. Saul was admitting he was in a mess and needed to hear from God who was not talking to him. If the Lord is not speaking to you, examine your heart and address the spiritual issues. He will speak if you are prepared to listen and obey.

Saul had put the mediums and spiritists out of the land in obedience to the directive of God in Deuteronomy 18:9-13. God has always warned His people against that particular kind of guidance, for when people consult palm readers, fortune tellers, and those who conduct seances, they are trafficking in demons. Therefore, the witches were either killed or put away when Saul had obeyed and rid the land of those who practiced such abominations. Because Saul was not hearing from God, he decided to find somebody who could communicate with the spirit world. He began looking for a witch.

> 7 Then Saul said to his servants, "Find me a woman who is a medium that I may go to her and inquire of her. And his servants said to him, In fact, there is a woman who is a medium at Endor. 8 So Saul disguised himself and put on other clothes, and he went, and two men with him; and they came to the woman by night. And he said, "Please conduct a séance for me, and bring up for me the one I shall name to you."

> 9 Then the woman said to him, "Look, you know what Saul has done, how he has cut off the mediums and the spiritists from the land. Why then do you lay a snare for my life, to cause me to die?"

> 10 And Saul swore to her by the Lord, saying, "As the Lord lives, no punishment shall come upon you for

this thing. [11] Then the woman said, "Whom shall I bring up for you? And he said, "Bring up Samuel for me" (1 Samuel 28:7-11).

Here was a woman who obviously had conversations with spirits and demons. Demons observe and sometimes control human behaviors. It is easy for them to deceive and give information through mediums about the lives of those persons they have either observed, influenced, or controlled. They inhabit people who aren't surrendered to Christ, with every intention of controlling someone's behavior in the future.

To help do so, they can have one of their sources tell us what so-and-so is going to do because they have good relationships with so-and-so and then try to bring it to pass. The problem is God clearly said that we are not to seek any information about the spirit world from any source other than His Holy Spirit and His word.

Therefore, you need to stay away from your neighborhood palm reader, tarot card reader, friendly astrologist, personal séance guru, psychic network, and all other sources of counterfeit guidance and information. They look attractive whenever we see them on television. They promise to hook us up with Mr. Right or Miss Sweet Thing. When we consult with them, we are walking on dangerous ground. When we go to those people trying to find out what is going to happen in the future or who we are going to be with, we are asking for trouble.

God is warning you that they are getting their information from demonic sources and to stay away from them. Are you surprised whenever a psychic leads the police to a hidden dead body? The demon saw the murder and they know where the body is. People are impressed and say, "Oh my goodness, this spirit world thing is real." They are trying to control and influence human behavior. They have people under their control, so they have every intention of having that person come to you next Friday and say everything the psychic said they were going to say. If you're not careful, you start giving your money there instead of into the Kingdom.

This witch had every intention of having one of her demons say things Samuel might have said for Saul's benefit. That was what she was planning to do. That's why you see the term "familiar spirit" used in that situation. That spirit is communicating with a spirit with which they are familiar. She was about to work her deception on Saul, and she was deceived as well. When we get caught up in this, we are deceived too. We think we know what we are doing but we are under the influence of the powers of darkness.

> [12] When the woman saw Samuel, she cried out with a loud voice. And the woman spoke to Saul, saying, "Why have you deceived me? For you are Saul!" [13] And the king said to her, "Do not be afraid. What did you see?" And the woman said to Saul, "I saw a spirit ascending out of the earth." [14] So he said to her, "What is his form?" And she said, "An old man is coming up, and he is covered with a mantle." And Saul perceived that it was Samuel, and he stooped with his face to the ground and bowed down (1 Samuel 28:12-14).

Samuel said to Saul, "Why have you disturbed me by bringing me up?" I can imagine Samuel saying "I was enjoying myself in Paradise and you have me coming back here to mess with you! You should have listened to me when you had the chance." Saul answered,

> "I am deeply distressed for the Philistines are making war against me, God has departed from me and does not answer me anymore, neither through prophets nor dreams. Therefore I've called you that you may reveal to me what I should do" (1 Samuel 28:15).

Scripture warns against and condemns every attempt to gain information from the spirit world apart from communing with God the Father, in the name of God the Son, by the guidance of God the Holy Spirit. All we need to know about what's happening and what will happen comes from God and His word. God will let you know what you need to know about your future. There are some things about your future you have no business knowing. It would scare you to death if you did know. You ought to be glad God doesn't tell you everything.

What if one day Jesus had told His disciples, "Follow me. James, but you're going to get your head cut off in a couple years. Peter, you're going to be crucified upside down. John, you're going to be tortured and boiled in oil and exiled to the island of Patmos. Philip, they're going to tie you to four horses and send them off into four different directions.'"?

We may not even be talking about those disciples today if the Lord had told them everything concerning their future before they were ready to follow Him even to the point of suffering and death. After they had walked with Him for a while and been assured that He was God in His flesh and their eternity was secure, then they could embrace the truth of "absent from the body, then immediately present with the Lord" (see 2 Corinthians 5:8).

You don't want to know certain things about your future before you are ready to embrace them. If God said next Tuesday at 6:35 PM you are going to be in a fatal car accident, you could not enjoy from now until Tuesday. You would not even get in the car on Tuesday. We should not want to know what He doesn't want us to know. *Guide me, lead me, moment by moment step-by-step into eternity.* I believe it was Woody Allen who said, "I don't mind dying, I just don't want to be there when it happens."

The woman was expecting one of her familiar demons and Samuel appeared and nearly scared her to death. Samuel said to Saul "Why do you consult me, now that the Lord has departed from you and become your enemy?" Those are words you never want to hear. How sad for King Saul that the last communication he received from the Lord through Samuel included the words stating God was his enemy.

Many commentaries on First Samuel claim that this speaker was a demonic spirit. With all due respect, please look at verse 16. The author of First Samuel, inspired by the Holy Spirit, clearly stated that *Samuel said*. That should answer any question whether or not it was Samuel speaking. God allowed him to come back from Paradise to give this message of judgment to Saul.

[17] The Lord has done what he predicted through me. The Lord has torn the kingdom out of your hands and given it to one of your neighbors—to David. [18] Because you did not obey the Lord or carry out his fierce wrath against the Amalekites, the Lord has done this to you today. [19] Moreover, the Lord will deliver

both Israel and you into the hands of the Philistines, and tomorrow you and your sons will be with me. The Lord will also give the army of Israel into the hands of the Philistines" (1 Samuel 28:17-19).

Saul wanted to hear from Samuel, hoping to get some good news and a plan outlining how to beat the Philistines. Instead, Samuel said that tomorrow he and his sons would be dead. Do you think Saul regretted his visit to the witch of Endor? All we need to know about the future is revealed in Scripture. It's explained to us as needed in the moment by the Holy Spirit. Avoid at all cost any other predictors of your future.

I stopped looking in the local paper to see what is supposed to be happening for Leos or Geminis. I don't call the psychic network. I don't go to palm readers and card readers. I study Revelation, Thessalonians, Daniel, and Zechariah. I know what's going to happen in the future. We reign and rule with Jesus Christ forever.

I will listen a little bit to what the weather man thinks is going to happen tomorrow. The only thing I know for sure about the future is what the word of God says. Anything else, I can do without. Samuel told Saul that his constant disobedience was going to cost him his life on the next day.

[20] Immediately Saul fell full length on the ground, filled with fear because of Samuel's words. His strength was gone, for he had eaten nothing all that day and all that night.

[21] When the woman came to Saul and saw that he was severely troubled, she said, "Look, your servant has obeyed you. I took my life in my hands and did what you told me to do. [22] Now please listen to your servant and let me give you some food so you may eat and have the strength to go on your way. He refused and said, "I will not eat." [23] But his servants joined the woman in urging him, and he listened to them. He got up from the ground and sat on the couch.

[24] The woman had a fattened calf at her house, which she butchered at once. She took some flour, kneaded it and baked bread without yeast. [25] Then she set it

before Saul and his men, and they ate. That same night they got up and left (1 Samuel 28:20-25).

Saul was a man who had every opportunity to listen to the Holy Spirit and didn't. All he did was worry about the kingdom of Saul instead of the kingdom of God. He got in a bind and what did he want? He wanted the Lord to talk to him. You know the Bible says, "Be not deceived, God is not mocked. Whatever a man sows, that shall he reap" (Galatians 6:7). God does not have to bail you out every time you get in a bind. You can keep ignoring Him if you wan, but you are going to cry out. You are going to cry out and He is going to be distant. You'll get a busy signal (see Proverbs 1:24-31).

SEEK GOD'S VOICE, NOT THE ENEMY'S

God says today if you hear His voice, don't harden your heart (see Hebrews 4:7). He loves to speak and communicate, but beloved, He is Lord. That means when He speaks, you are obligated to obey. He may let you choose your sin, but you don't get to choose your consequences.

God is faithful to rescue us from the traps we fall into while we are stumbling in darkness. We have the word and Spirit of God, and His word is a light unto our feet. We have all the light we need for our journey but we still stumble in the darkness because we don't always listen as well as we should. In chapter 29, we read,

> ¹ Then the Philistines gathered together all their armies at Aphek, and the Israelites encamped by a fountain which is in Jezreel. ² And the lords of the Philistines passed in review by hundreds and by thousands, but David and his men passed in review at the rear with King Achish. ³ Then the princes of the Philistines said, "What are these Hebrews doing here? Achish said to the princes of the Philistines, "Is this not David, the servant of Saul king of Israel, who has been with me these days, or these years? And to this day I have found no fault in him since he defected to me."
>
> ⁴ But the princes of the Philistines were angry with him; so the princes of the Philistines said to him,

"Make this fellow return, that he may go back to the place which you have appointed for him, and do not let him go down with us to battle, lest in the battle he become our adversary. For with what could he reconcile himself to his master, if not with the heads of these men? [5] Is this not David, of whom they sang to one another in dances, saying: 'Saul has slain his thousands, And David his ten thousands'?" (1 Samuel 29:1-5).

It is an embarrassing position to be in when someone asks what we are doing when we are where we should not be. The Philistines were about to go into battle and they were being reviewed by their commander who saw a band of Hebrews about to go into battle with them. Those soldiers asked what those Hebrews were doing in their army. They wanted to know whether or not, in the midst of the battle, the Israelites would suddenly change sides and renew their loyalty to their home country and help Israel defeat them. Why was the renowned Israeli military leader serving with their troops? As I looked at this passage, it made me think of some embarrassing times in my life when someone had "put me in check" and asked what I was doing where I was. I was out of place.

Have you ever been the only believer at a place where drinks are flowing and the smoke fills the room and you are having what you think is a good time and somebody who knows you asks why you are there? Are you representing Christ well at that moment, or have you ignored the voice of God because you were depressed, discouraged, or defeated?

The good news is God loves you. He may have somebody like that to help you get back to where you should be. Many of the believers need to be rescued from the enemy's camp because of poor choices they have made along the way. Even when we are powerless to free ourselves, He remains powerful and can deliver us.

Then Achish called David and said to him, "Surely, as the Lord lives, you have been upright, and your going out and your coming in with me in the army is good in my sight. For to this day I have not found evil in you since the day of your coming to me. Nevertheless the lords do not favor you" (1 Samuel 29:6).

David had been living in deception, killing Philistines while he had the king of Philistia thinking he was being a good soldier.

> [7] Therefore return now and go in peace, that you may not displease the lords of the Philistines."

> [8] So David said to Achish, "But what have I done? And to this day what have you found in your servant as long as I have been with you, that I may not go and fight against the enemies of my lord the king? Don't you trust me by now?" (1 Samuel 29:7-8).

If you keep lying over a long period of time, it starts to feel natural, doesn't it? This was a man who loved the Lord, but this is what happens when we get in one of those valleys and we can't get out by ourselves.

> [10] Now therefore, rise early in the morning with your master's servants who have come with you. And as soon as you are up early in the morning and have light, depart." [11] So David and his men rose early to depart in the morning, to return to the land of the Philistines. And the Philistines went up to Jezreel (1 Samuel 29:10-11).

David was not back home yet but at least God had spared him from getting in deeper trouble than he already was. We should stop and think about all those times when our choices took us down or trapped us, and we said, "Lord, I don't see how I can get out of this." God has power to rescue you, doesn't He?

If you're struggling to hear His voice today because you are depressed, walking through darkness, or drowning in deception, I challenge you to remember the promises of God. Trust Him to keep His word. You can experience joy instead of discouragement, light instead of darkness, and truth instead of deception. Jesus can set you free. No matter the situation in which you find yourself, listen and be ready to obey. Watch God work on your behalf.

Father, we pray that we would never doubt Your love and guidance as we go through the seasons of life that might be discouraging or depressing. You have promised to never leave us or forsake us, and we ask Your Spirit to remind us of that precious truth whenever we need to be reminded. We pray we would never seek to gain spiritual guidance from any source other than your Word, Your Spirit, and those who speak in accordance with what You have already chosen to reveal in Scripture. Thank You for revealing to us all we need to know about life beyond the grave through the resurrection of our Lord and Savior Jesus Christ. Give us the courage to stay out of the enemy's camp, and to always be able to live in such a way that our allegiance to You is not questioned. In Jesus' name we pray, Amen.

FROM UNBEARABLE PAIN TO UNSPEAKABLE JOY

Have you ever been in a situation that seemed like your worst nightmare had come true? Were your own decisions the reason why everything had gone horribly wrong? Did you turn to the Lord for comfort, or did you lose your passion for life and immerse yourself in guilt and self-condemnation?

Israel and Amalek had a history of being enemies with one another. The hostility traces back to the time when Israel was moving through the wilderness and the Amalekites attacked them from behind, where the elderly and frail were most likely to be. The Lord made sure Israel never forgot that merciless hostility:

> "Remember what the Amalekites did to you on the journey after you left Egypt. They met you along the way and attacked all your stragglers from behind when you were tired and weary. They did not fear God" (Deuteronomy 25:17-18).

The Lord reminded Israel to completely blot out Amalek but King Saul failed to do so, deciding instead to show off the king of Amalek as a conquered foe. In a poignant example of why we should completely obey every directive from our Lord, King Saul would eventually die on the battlefield at the hands of his Amalekite foe. Likewise, whenever we choose to partially defeat an issue the Lord directs us to crucify, we set ourselves up for a repeat attack that could be devastating.

Just as the Amalekites were always looking to attack the Israelites, our spiritual enemy is also looking for every chance to attack us, which is the reason we need to guard our hearts and homes from his vengeful attacks. Satan and his hordes of demons have no qualms about attacking any weak or struggling believer, or trying to find any area of vulnerability in our lives.

First Samuel 30 opens with David still in a compromised

position, pretending to be loyal to the Philistine army. The Amalekites had raided the city of Ziklag, destroying it and taking captive the women and children. David and his men returned to find their loved ones missing, not knowing what fate had befallen them. The Lord will not hesitate to orchestrate events to get us back into alignment with His will for our lives. We should expect potentially painful consequences that accompany our disobedience.

> [1] Now it happened, when David and his men came to Ziklag, on the third day, that the Amalekites had invaded the South and Ziklag, attacked Ziklag and burned it with fire, [2] and had taken captive the women and those who were there, from small to great; they did not kill anyone, but carried them away and went their way. [3] So David and his men came to the city, and there it was, burned with fire; and their wives, their sons, and their daughters had been taken captive. [4] Then David and the people who were with him lifted up their voices and wept, until they had no more power to weep. [5] And David's two wives, Ahinoam the Jezreelitess, and Abigail the widow of Nabal the Carmelite, had been taken captive. [6] Now David was greatly distressed, for the people spoke of stoning him, because the soul of all the people was grieved, every man for his sons and his daughters. But David strengthened himself in the Lord his God (1 Samuel 30:1-6).

David's men were understandably overcome with grief, and the text says they wept until they were too exhausted to cry any longer. Can you imagine the kind of emotional pain that caused trained soldiers and combat veterans to cry themselves into weakness? What happened next should not be a surprise to any leader who has been responsible for a decision that caused others to lose things of value. The men who had been protecting David were so angry that they were ready to stone him to death.

Only our Lord Jesus Christ can carry us through such painful times, and David found strength to go on by leaning on the Lord. There will be many times in life when it seems your world is falling apart. The road to recovery begins when you learn how to encourage yourself in the Lord. As you read this account of David's actions, I trust you are learning how to draw strength and comfort from the Lord, especially during those times when you seem not to have a friend to depend on.

As I reflect on the pain and trauma of this scenario and how David must have felt, my mind is drawn to the words he penned in Psalm 22:1 when he wrote, "My God, My God, why have you forsaken me"? How many times he must have felt forsaken when he was being chased by Saul and living in caves. Did David feel God had forsaken him again because the Lord did not protect his wives and children while he was out conducting raids?

When our Lord Jesus was paying the ultimate price for our sins while hanging on the cross, He uttered these same words when He experienced being forsaken by the Father. We do not have the capacity to comprehend how horrific that moment of terror must have been to our sinless Savior, who knew no sin but became sin for us. A supernatural darkness prevented sinful observers from fully witnessing this holy transaction, while Jesus endured God's wrath against sin, a loneliness no believer will ever have to experience. His amazing display of love has gifted us with eternal companionship with our God and fellow believers.

> [7] Then David said to Abiathar the priest, Ahimelech's son, "Please bring the ephod here to me." And Abiathar brought the ephod to David. [8] So David inquired of the Lord, saying, "Shall I pursue this troop? Shall I overtake them?" And He answered him, "Pursue, for you shall surely overtake them and without fail recover all." [9] So David went, he and the six hundred men who were with him, and came to the Brook Besor, where those stayed who were left behind. [10] But David pursued, he and four hundred men; for two hundred stayed behind, who were so weary that they could not cross the Brook Besor. [11] Then they found an Egyptian in the field, and brought him to David; and they gave him bread and he ate, and they let him drink water. [12] And they gave him a piece of a cake of figs and two clusters of raisins. So when he

had eaten, his strength came back to him; for he had eaten no bread nor drunk water for three days and three nights. [13] Then David said to him, "To whom do you belong, and where are you from?" And he said, "I am a young man from Egypt, servant of an Amalekite; and my master left me behind, because three days ago I fell sick. [14] We made an invasion of the southern area of the Cherethites, in the territory which belongs to Judah, and of the southern area of Caleb; and we burned Ziklag with fire." [15] And David said to him, "Can you take me down to this troop?" So he said, "Swear to me by God that you will neither kill me nor deliver me into the hands of my master, and I will take you down to this troop" (1 Samuel 30:7-15).

I find this story provides one of the greatest examples of relational leadership we have in Scripture. The same men who were devastated by the apparent loss of everyone near and dear to them, largely due to the decisions of their leader, again chose to follow him into battle. I suggest that David's communion with the Lord was instrumental in God moving on their hearts to once again join the fight. Do you believe our God will answer you as clearly as He did David during this incident? If not, why not? This is a great lesson for leaders since none of us are immune to poor decisions, and we should be grateful that God continues to move on the hearts of men and women to respond to our oft-flawed leadership.

As David followed the instruction of the Lord, he was able to go in pursuit of the enemy that had taken captive their loved ones. In the providence of God, David and his company encountered a young Egyptian man who had been abandoned by his Amalekite slave masters due to failing health. David and his company provided life-giving sustenance to him in exchange for his willingness to lead them to where their families had been taken captive. This historical incident is yet another verification of the unique ways our Lord guides us when we are doing His will.

What were the odds of David and his men accidentally encountering a person, discarded because he could no longer serve his master, who was in the right place at the right time and able to give them exactly what they needed? The young Egyptian received assurance from David that he would not be turned over to the Amalekites after providing help for them. In similar fashion, Satan takes people captive, uses and misuses them, and then leaves them to suffer if they are no longer effective for him. Rest assured, if you have been abandoned as this Egyptian was and come to Christ for help as this young man came to David, you will receive life-giving nourishment and not be given back to the evil one who held you captive.

> [16] And when he had brought him down, there they were, spread out over all the land, eating and drinking and dancing, because of all the great spoil which they had taken from the land of the Philistines and from the land of Judah. [17] Then David attacked them from twilight until the evening of the next day. Not a man of them escaped, except four hundred young men who rode on camels and fled. [18] So David recovered all that the Amalekites had carried away, and David rescued his two wives. [19] And nothing of theirs was lacking, either small or great, sons or daughters, spoil or anything which they had taken from them; David recovered all. [20] Then David took all the flocks and herds they had driven before those other livestock, and said, "This is David's spoil" (1 Samuel 30:16-20).

Thanks to the guidance from the Egyptian young man, David and his men found the raiding armies that had taken captive their loved ones. David's men conquered them and safely recovered their families and belongings, returning home and reuniting with the men who had been left behind due to weariness. It is nothing short of miraculous to notice that everything and every person that had been taken captive were recovered.

As we grow in our trust of the Lord, we will have times of recovering certain things or relationships that once appeared to be lost forever. This principle aligns with what our Lord spoke through the prophet Joel when He told the Israelites He would restore to them the years that the swarming locusts had eaten (see Joel 2:25). We should not be so swift to give up hope once we come to know the God of hope, since He does the impossible on a regular basis.

21 Now David came to the two hundred men who had been so weary that they could not follow David, whom they also had made to stay at the Brook Besor. So they went out to meet David and to meet the people who were with him. And when David came near the people, he greeted them.

22 Then all the wicked and worthless men of those who went with David answered and said, "Because they did not go with us, we will not give them any of the spoil that we have recovered, except for every man's wife and children, that they may lead them away and depart." 23 But David said, "My brethren, you shall not do so with what the LORD has given us, who has preserved us and delivered into our hand the troop that came against us. 24 For who will heed you in this matter? But as his part is who goes down to the battle, so shall his part be who stays by the supplies; they shall share alike." 25 So it was, from that day forward; he made it a statute and an ordinance for Israel to this day. 26 Now when David came to Ziklag, he sent some of the spoil to the elders of Judah, to his friends, saying, "Here is a present for you from the spoil of the enemies of the Lord"—27 to those who were in Bethel, those who were in Ramoth of the South, those who were in Jattir, 28 those who were in Aroer, those who were in Siphmoth, those who were in Eshtemoa, 29 those who were in Rachal, those who were in the cities of the Jerahmeelites, those who were in the cities of the Kenites, 30 those who were in Hormah, those who were in Chorashan, those who were in Athach, 31 those who were in Hebron, and to all the places where David himself and his men were accustomed to rove (1 Samuel 30:21-31).

Some of the soldiers who had engaged in the battle did not want to share the spoils of victory with those who had not gone with them to the front lines of battle. David again demonstrated godly leadership skills and exemplary teamwork principles by mandating that the ones who stayed behind would share equally with those who went to the front lines.

An abiding spiritual principle from this story is that we often fail to give credit to those persons who stay behind and pray for the ones who are most visible in ministry. The public victories that take place are always connected to those persons who are behind the scenes spending time in prayer. As church leaders, we must never fail to acknowledge those persons who are faithful in prayer, often invisible to the masses, but highly visible to the One who hears and answers prayer. David wisely distributed the spoils of victory to all the cities that had provided refuge for his team as he went through this painful season of his journey to the throne of Israel (see 1 Samuel 30:26-31).

Godly leaders should follow this example by remembering the people and places God used in their lives to get them through the difficult seasons that comprised their moving towards maturity in their walk with Christ. Victory is always a team effort, and we must do a better job of making everyone around us feel appreciated for the role they play as we all advance the Kingdom.

> *Father, we bless Your name and praise You for who you are. Thank You for restoring to us so much more than we had lost through the faithless choices we are prone to make. Thank You for allowing us to share in Your victories, even when we were too weary to stay on the frontlines of the battlefield. Encourage us to stay prayerful for others who are fighting to advance the Kingdom and rescue the lost, and remind us that there are no coincidences in our lives, but only divine appointments as we encounter those persons You have put in place to help us on our journey to grow closer to You. We praise You in Jesus' name, Amen.*

A Sad Ending to What Could Have Been a Different Story

¹ Now the Philistines fought against Israel; and the men of Israel fled from before the Philistines, and fell slain on Mount Gilboa. ² Then the Philistines followed hard after Saul and his sons. And the Philistines killed Jonathan, Abinadab, and Malchishua, Saul's sons. ³ The battle became fierce against Saul. The archers hit him, and he was severely wounded by the archers. ⁴ Then Saul said to his armorbearer, "Draw your sword, and thrust me through with it, lest these uncircumcised men come and thrust me through and abuse me." But his armorbearer would not, for he was greatly afraid. Therefore Saul took a sword and fell on it. ⁵ And when his armorbearer saw that Saul was dead, he also fell on his sword, and died with him. ⁶ So Saul, his three sons, his armorbearer, and all his men died together that same day. ⁷ And when the men of Israel who were on the other side of the valley, and those who were on the other side of the Jordan, saw that the men of Israel had fled and that Saul and his sons were dead, they forsook the cities and fled; and the Philistines came and dwelt in them.

⁸ So it happened the next day, when the Philistines came to strip the slain, that they found Saul and his three sons fallen on Mount Gilboa. ⁹ And they cut off his head and stripped off his armor, and sent word throughout the land of the Philistines, to proclaim it in the temple of their idols and among the people. ¹⁰ Then they put his armor in the temple of the Ashtoreths, and they fastened his body to the wall

of Beth Shan. [11] Now when the inhabitants of Jabesh Gilead heard what the Philistines had done to Saul, [12] all the valiant men arose and traveled all night, and took the body of Saul and the bodies of his sons from the wall of Beth Shan; and they came to Jabesh and burned them there. [13] Then they took their bones and buried them under the tamarisk tree at Jabesh, and fasted seven days (1 Samuel 31:1-13).

First Samuel Chapter 31 opens with a description of the Philistines fighting against the Israelites, and the account of Saul's sons (Jonathan, Abinadab, and Malchishua) being killed in battle. King Saul was struck by an archer's arrow, suffering a wound that he knew was fatal. He asked his armor bearer to hasten his death by sword so the Philisitine army would not abuse him when they executed him. His armor bearer could not bring himself to do that to his king, so Saul fell on his own sword to hasten his death. In an act of grief and loyalty, Saul's armor bearer chose to die in the same manner. It was a tragic day of loss for Israel.

Saul's life must be regarded as an epic failure with many wasted opportunities to bring glory to God. He was more interested in his own kingdom than the one that is eternal. Saul was given every resource he needed to be successful as a leader, but he refused to trust the Lord or honor Him. Like some today, he would seek God's counsel only when things were going wrong and follow his own instincts when he felt a situation was manageable. Do you have areas in your life that sound like those of this ignominious king of Israel?

When we looked at 1 Samuel 14, I mentioned the concept of a sinkhole. Occasionally on the news, I have seen large sinkholes that opened and literally swallowed cars or homes. A surface that once looked solid was exposed to be weak and faulty underneath, and the sudden manifestation of the sinkhole brought devastating results. Saul's pride was a sinkhole in his heart, and eventually it swallowed him up and led to his downfall—along with that of many others. Hopefully, you are guarding your own heart from a similar fate. If the Holy Spirit is speaking to you about something you need to address, now is a good time to take whatever steps necessary to prevent a future disaster in your walk with Christ.

The Lord Jesus said that "many are called, but few are chosen" (Matthew 20:16). We need to recognize that the word for *chosen* can also be understood as *choice* or *prime*, a term we use to acknowledge high quality. I like grade A choice steaks and other meats that measure up to being labeled as choice—better than average and of the highest quality. The Apostle Paul was a chosen or choice vessel, because the Lord knew Paul would give his all to advance the Kingdom. The parents of Saul of Tarsus, also Benjamites like Saul, likely took the name for their son from this abysmal king who never lived up to the standards of being a choice servant of the Lord. He was called and anointed, but he refused to surrender his kingdom to the real King of Israel, the Lord God Almighty. Saul of Tarsus, who became the Apostle Paul, redeemed the tribal name of Saul and did what the king centuries before him chose not to do—walk in God's will for his life.

King Saul did not live to feel the abuse of the Philistines, but they certainly abused his corpse after his suicide on the battlefield. Just as young David had once taken off the head of the Philistine champion Goliath (see 1 Samuel 17), the Philistine soldiers cut off the head of King Saul. They stripped him of his armor, taking it and Saul's body to their pagan temples to hang as a display of their victory. When the men of Jabesh Gilead heard of the atrocities done to Saul's body, they took a risk and retrieved the bodies of Saul and his sons, burning them and burying their bones as they grieved for seven days (see 1 Samuel 31:8-13)

Saul was a man who was the people's choice because of his physical stature, but he looked better on the outside than he was on the inside. He was insecure about a lot of things, insanely jealous, envious, and threatened by a young man who was actually honored to serve under him. One of the things I wish every believer would embrace is that we can be secure in Christ, both for salvation and also in whatever ministry He calls us to. There is no need to be threatened by the gifts and charisma of others when you are doing what God has called you to do.

Saul's decisions cost him his life and those of his sons, depriving his descendants a chance to legitimately occupy the throne of Israel. David also made some poor decisions, and yet his sons would have the privilege of ruling the nation as their progenitor had done. What was the difference? David set his heart to pursue the Lord and honor Him as the true King of Israel. There is a world of difference between making mistakes while being on the right road as opposed to making poor choices while traveling on the wrong road. The path King Saul had chosen was never going to arrive at the right destination. David made his journey more difficult than it should have been, but the Spirit of God continued to keep him on the right path.

Saul's death did not benefit others and his life was not the blessing it could have been. The Messiah of Israel and Savior of the world is a physical descendant of King David. The death of our Lord Jesus Christ benefits everyone who believes. Saul died because he had no hope. Jesus died and rose again, and He has provided a living hope and eternal life to all who believe. Your kingdom will come and go quickly. His is eternal. Who sits on the throne of your life is not a game, but has the most serious and lasting implications. The question posed to you is the same one posed to Saul and everyone since: Your kingdom come or His? Have you given up ruling yours so you can enjoy living under His rule forever?

Father, we bless Your Name and praise You for who You are. Thank You for restoring to us so much more than we had lost through the faithless choices we were prone to make. Thank You for allowing us to share in Your victories, even when we were too weary to stay on the frontlines of the battlefield. We pray that we would never give up hope while we keep our eyes on You, and that You would be glorified by how we live and how we die. We also pray that we would learn to seek Your guidance in every decision we make. May Your kingdom come and Your will be done on earth as it is in heaven, in Jesus' name we pray, amen.

EPILOGUE

The writer of Hebrews said believers are receiving a kingdom that cannot be shaken (see Hebrews 12:28). The Kingdom referred to is not of our own doing because everything about our own little kingdoms is shaky. Many people continue to build their own little kingdoms upon a foundation that cannot stand the test of time or eternity. Anytime we attempt to build anything on a foundation other than the solid Rock known as the Lord Jesus Christ, collapse is just a matter of time (see Luke 6:46-49).

They refuse to step down from the throne, acting like life is a game they play to see who can win, instead of a partnership with the Lord of the universe Something inside us wants to have everything under control, and it feels good to be in charge of a life that is going well. As we have been reminded through this book, however, we are destined to be kings and queens, but not of our own kingdoms. All who have bowed their knees and surrendered their lives to the Lord and Savior Jesus Christ will inherit a kingdom forever. It is His kingdom over which He is King, but it is tailor-made for us to enjoy because He drew us to Himself and we responded to His grace, mercy, and love.

Jesus prayed, "Thy Kingdom come, thy will be done, on earth, as it is in Heaven" (Matthew 6:10) as I mentioned in the Introduction. Is that really your prayer of anticipation or just words you have been taught to repeat? Jesus was all about the Kingdom and the Jews knew it and most were not happy. They had built their own kingdom of rule-keeping and legalism, just like countless others have done through the ages. Even Pilate recognized what was going on in the dispute between the Jews and Jesus and he wrote it on the marker above Jesus' crucified body: "Jesus Christ, King of the Jews" and had it written in three languages for all to read and understand. The Jews were offended because they did not recognize or serve Jesus' kingdom. Are you offended too or will you acknowledge that Pilate's declaration was true and Jesus is worthy of all your allegiance, not just on Sunday but every day and in every way?

I pray you will come to fully live out the truth Paul wrote in his letter to the Colossian church:

For this reason we also, since the day we heard it, do not cease to pray for you, and to ask that you may be filled with the knowledge of His will in all wisdom and spiritual understanding; that you may walk worthy of the Lord, fully pleasing Him, being fruitful in every good work and increasing in the knowledge of God; strengthened with all might, according to His glorious power, for all patience and longsuffering with joy; giving thanks to the Father who has qualified us to be partakers of the inheritance of the saints in the light. *He has delivered us from the power of darkness and conveyed us into the kingdom of the Son of His love, in whom we have redemption through His blood, the forgiveness of sins* (Colossians 1:9-14, emphasis added).

As you answer the question in the byline of this book, *Yours or His Kingdom Come?,* I urge you to declare your allegiance to His kingdom and then live out your life as a citizen of that Kingdom, with all the rights and responsibilities thereof. Thy Kingdom come, Lord Jesus!

DR. RON MORRISON BIO

Rev. Ronald J. Morrison (D. Min. from Alliance Theological Seminary) is the founding and senior pastor of Hope Alliance Bible Church, which he planted in 1995 after 21 years of working as a factory laborer for the Lincoln Electric Company in Cleveland, Ohio. He is a lifelong resident of Greater Cleveland and served in the U.S. Army from 1971-1973. Ron met Anita Bivens in 1978 while she was attending the Ohio State University, and they have been married since December of 1979. Anita holds an M.Ed. from John Carroll University.

Ron has served on the board of directors of the Christian and Missionary Alliance for sixteen years and was chairman from 2005-2009. He and Anita have been featured speakers at C&MA Christian colleges and at field forums in Brazil, Japan, and Taiwan. He currently serves as the Urban Ministries Coach for the Central District of the C&MA, and on the Licensing Committee.

Ron has been an instructor for Moody Bible Institute since 2005, and his church is the host site for Moody programs in Cleveland. He was a distance learning student of Moody Bible Institute while working in the factory, which is why he encourages others not to let anything hinder the pursuit of a biblical education. He has also served as an adjunct professor for Crown College and South University. He has a heart for teaching, coaching, and mentoring aspiring urban leaders. Ron is also the co-founder and president of Alliance for Family Hope, Inc., a community development corporation formed in 2008 to educate, encourage, and enrich the under-served children and families in Southeast Cleveland.

Ron is a student and practitioner of expository preaching that leads to transformation and involvement in ministry. He is also determined to bring high quality education to those who have limited access to it.

Dr. Ron Morrison can be reached at:

Hope Alliance Bible Church
5050 Stanley Avenue
Maple Heights, Ohio 44137-2825

216.581.2084

www.hopealliancebiblechurch.org

hopealliance@sbcglobal.net